"As a psychologist and lifelong music synthesize these two passions to hel and Bonavitacola outline many effective and practical ways to creatively weave music into DBT! You do not need to be a musician or a psychologist to find these therapeutic activities immediately applicable to your patients, students, and colleagues practicing DBT."

—*Alec L. Miller, PsyD, Co-Founder and Clinical Director of CBC, White Plains, NY, and Clinical Professor of Psychiatry and Behavioral Sciences, Albert Einstein College of Medicine*

"*Creative DBT Activities Using Music* is a refreshing and stimulating read, providing key information and unique insight when utilizing music- and art-focused DBT techniques. As an experienced music therapist and educator, Deborah Spiegel has opened a 'DBT door' to readers and laid a foundation ensuring informed and individualized treatment in the therapy field and beyond."

—*Katherine E. Borst, MT-BC, board-certified music therapist*

"Spiegel, Makary, and Bonavitacola have compiled an impressive collection of music-related activities designed to 'teach, strengthen, and anchor' DBT and other life skills. This book shows how to use music and music appreciation in the DBT skills curriculum. The authors provide creativity and inspiration from the field of music therapy. Well done!"

—*Cedar Koons, DBT consultant, researcher, DBT-LBC certified therapist, and author of* The Mindfulness Solution for Intense Emotions: Take Control of Borderline Personality Disorder with DBT

"During my time working with adolescents I've found music really engages them, and when kids are engaged that's half the battle for teaching them skills. Especially at a program like mine where group participation is expected as part of treatment."

—*Libby Arsenault, DBT skills group leader, mental health counselor at an inpatient DBT program, and non-musician*

Creative DBT Activities
Using Music

of related interest

DBT-Informed Art Therapy
Mindfulness, Cognitive Behavior Therapy, and the Creative Process
Susan M. Clark
ISBN 978 1 84905 733 2
eISBN 978 1 78450 103 7

DBT Therapeutic Activity Ideas for Working with Teens
Skills and Exercises for Working with Clients with Borderline Personality
Disorder, Depression, Anxiety, and Other Emotional Sensitivities
Carol Lozier
ISBN 978 1 78592 785 0
eISBN 978 1 78450 718 3

A Comprehensive Guide to Music Therapy, 2nd Edition
Theory, Clinical Practice, Research and Training
Edited by Stine Lindahl Jacobsen, Inge Nygaard Pedersen, and Lars Ole Bonde
Foreword by Helen Odell-Miller
ISBN 978 1 78592 427 9
eISBN 978 1 78450 793 0

Raising Self-Esteem in Adults
An Eclectic Approach with Art Therapy, CBT and DBT Based Techniques
Susan I. Buchalter
ISBN 978 1 84905 966 4
eISBN 978 0 85700 821 3

CREATIVE DBT ACTIVITIES USING MUSIC

Interventions for Enhancing Engagement
and Effectiveness in Therapy

Deborah Spiegel
with Suzanne Makary
and Lauren Bonavitacola

Jessica Kingsley Publishers
London and Philadelphia

A version of this work was published in 2010 under the title *Music Activities & More for Teaching DBT Skills and Enhancing Any Therapy: Even for the Non-Musician* by Deborah Spiegel (Authorhouse: *www.authorhouse.com*)

This edition published in 2020
by Jessica Kingsley Publishers
73 Collier Street
London N1 9BE, UK
and
400 Market Street, Suite 400
Philadelphia, PA 19106, USA

www.jkp.com

Library of Congress Cataloging in Publication Data
A CIP catalog record for this book is available from the Library of Congress

British Library Cataloguing in Publication Data
A CIP catalogue record for this book is available from the British Library

ISBN 978 1 78775 180 4
eISBN 978 1 78775 182 8

Printed and bound in the United States

Contents

2. WORKBOOK: FOR THE INDIVIDUAL TO LEARN AND PRACTICE DBT SKILLS IN A CREATIVE WAY WITH OR WITHOUT CLINICIAN GUIDANCE

About the Authors

Deborah Spiegel, MT-BC, is a board-certified music therapist who has been in the field since 1976, providing music therapy for people of all ages.

She was first introduced to Dialectical Behavior Therapy (DBT) in 2001 when she worked as an integral member of a DBT-based treatment team at the Colorado Mental Health Institute. She was trained in DBT alongside her treatment team, by representatives of Behavioral Tech.

Over the following 11 years Deborah developed a system of strengthening and generalizing DBT skills within her music therapy groups and in using music activities while teaching the DBT skills as a DBT skills group leader in her skills training groups.

Deborah's passion for DBT-informed music therapy led her to spearhead a research project to validate the effectiveness of DBT-informed music therapy. For updates on research regarding music therapy and DBT visit: dbtmusic.com.

Ms. Spiegel presented a two-day workshop for the rehabilitation therapy department in eight California State Hospitals in 2014–15 called "Supporting Patients in DBT through Rehabilitation Therapy." (This included music therapists, art therapists, dance therapists, recreation therapists, and occupational therapists.)

Prior to that, starting in 2011, she facilitated a similar workshop called "DBT: Practical Life Skills Reinforced through Music Therapy" for music therapists at Clifton T. Perkins Hospital Center in Maryland, Immaculata University in Pennsylvania, Eastern Michigan University, and a variety of other locations nationwide.

After her first online presentation of this class in February of 2012, what is now The Spiegel Academy was born. She is CEO and director of TheSpiegelAcademy.com, offering convenient, quality, and affordable online continuing education classes for music therapists and allied health professionals on a wide range of topics, including that original workshop.

Besides being a DBT-informed music therapist, Deborah Spiegel has a unique qualification: a certification in clinical hypnotherapy (since 1989), which adds depth to her guided imagery sessions. The process gives the recipients tools to help them connect with their own inner wisdom to bring about changes in their own lives. This informs the imagery scripts she has shared in this book. Deborah conducts imagery/hypnotherapy sessions in person or over the telephone or internet in her private practice. She often uses these to strengthen DBT skills.

Lauren Bonavitacola, PsyD, MT-BC, is a licensed psychologist, DBT-Linehan Board of Certification Certified Clinician™, and board-certified music therapist working for Cognitive & Behavioral Consultants of Westchester and Manhattan (CBC), an outpatient CBT- and DBT-based treatment, training, and consultation center. She is the Director of Trauma-Focused Treatment Programs at CBC and works with adolescents, adults, couples, and families.

Dr. Bonavitacola has expertise and specialized training in the delivery of evidence-based treatments for trauma, anxiety, mood, substance use, eating, and personality disorders across the lifespan. She specializes in the implementation of DBT for Borderline Personality Disorder (BPD) and associated conditions, as well as CBT for anxiety and mood disorders, particularly Post Traumatic Stress Disorder (PTSD) in adolescents and adults.

She received her bachelor's degree in Music Therapy and Music Performance with a minor in Psychology from the University of Miami, and she earned both her master's and doctorate in Clinical Psychology from Rutgers University Graduate School of Applied and Professional Psychology (GSAPP).

Additionally, Lauren consults to several school districts in New York on DBT implementation in schools as well as conducting trainings in house and at schools on DBT and CBT treatment implementation. She is a supervisor of pre-doctoral psychology externs and post-doctoral fellows at CBC. Dr. Bonavitacola also teaches and supervises for The Spiegel Academy's DBT-Informed Music Therapy Program.

Dr. Bonavitacola has published written works in several peer-reviewed journals and books and presented on topics related to CBT and DBT at national and international conferences including those sponsored by the Association for Behavioral and Cognitive Therapies (ABCT), the International Society for the Improvement and Teaching of Dialectical Behavior Therapy (ISITDBT), and the Anxiety and Depression Association of America (ADAA). She is an active member of both ABCT and ISITDBT.

Suzanne Makary, MT-BC, is a board-certified music therapist who has spent her career serving adults with mental health challenges. She completed her internship in 1997 at Allentown State Hospital. Since that opportunity, Suzanne has worked with an interdisciplinary team in the partial hospitalization setting.

Throughout her journey as a professional, Suzanne designs and leads daily music therapy groups to assist in learning and reaching wellness goals with her clients. She found Marsha Linehan's original text *Cognitive-Behavioral Treatment of Borderline Personality Disorder* inspiring and used concepts found in this text to help frame her work. In 2017, Suzanne completed the yearlong "DBT-Informed Music Therapy" program through The Spiegel Academy.

As a DBT-informed music therapist, Suzanne has created a curriculum for the Innovations Partial Hospital Program at St. Luke's University Health Network focused on teaching DBT skills daily.

Suzanne finds sharing ideas as professionals with one another and our clients to be rejuvenating. This text allowed her to do just that through contributing some of her original ideas and working with Deborah to expand the first edition.

Preface

Lauren Bonavitacola, PsyD, MT-BC

As an excited and motivated second-year psychology graduate student, I learned about the work of Deborah Spiegel at a training that she conducted at Immaculata University in Pennsylvania. I was studying clinical psychology at the Graduate School of Applied and Professional Psychology (GSAPP) at Rutgers University and had just started to dive deeper into my training and understanding of DBT under the direction of Shireen Rizvi, PhD, a former graduate student of the treatment developer herself, Marsha Linehan, PhD. Prior to graduate school, I had completed my undergraduate degree in music therapy and it was during my internship at a child and adolescent inpatient hospital that I was first introduced to DBT. I was pretty immediately drawn into its pragmatic nature and could easily see how this approach could be beneficial for the emotionally dysregulated teens I was working with at the hospital. I had always hoped that during graduate school and beyond I would find a way to integrate clinical psychology and music therapy; therefore, when I saw that Deborah had found a way to infuse music therapy interventions into the teaching of DBT, I was very intrigued! Attending this initial workshop marked the start of what would end up being a very rewarding and enriching professional relationship and collaboration.

As excited as I was about integrating music therapy into my work as a budding psychologist implementing DBT, I still had a lot of questions about this approach. Being indoctrinated into the world of evidence-based psychotherapies in graduate school instilled in me a deep desire to ensure that the work I was doing and the treatments I disseminated to others were based in a solid research base. Therefore from the beginning of my collaboration with Deborah, I wanted to know: where's the evidence? How do we know that incorporating music into the teaching of DBT will make a difference in client learning or generalization of these skills? Are there other variables that the addition of music impacts, such as level of engagement, that could enhance overall outcomes? My quest to answer these questions began.

I started by reviewing the music therapy literature. One of the most robust science-minded communities of researchers in the music therapy field would arguably be made up of those who hail from The Academy of Neurologic Music Therapy (NMT). Preeminent researchers including the late Robert Unkefer and Michael Thaut have expanded the literature in the realm of neurologic music therapy significantly, helping bring clout to this field and its evidence-based techniques that have been shown to improve so many functional behaviors. Within this literature exist many research studies demonstrating the effects of music on the brain and on various neurological and physiological processes including affect arousal and regulation, memory, language acquisition, pain perception, and sensorimotor development and rehabilitation to name a few. There are countless studies to cite, but several books and meta-analyses exist that summarize the literature nicely (Lee, 2016; Thaut, 2005; Thaut & Hoemberg, 2014; Pelletier, 2004). Additionally, the NMT Academy has a bibliography of the evidence base for its interventions located at: https://nmtacademy.co/supporting-research-by-technique.

It is not a far stretch to see the overlap in these areas with many of the goals of DBT skills training, for example:

- One of the aims of emotion regulation skills is to learn how to modulate emotion intensity, which can be achieved through music interventions.

- Mindfulness skills aim to help us have control over where we place our attention, which can reduce pain perception, as can music.

- Distress tolerance skills sometimes incorporate relaxation, which music can enhance.

- Mnemonic devices are used for so many DBT skills to facilitate memory of a skill, in the same way as musical mnemonic devices.

Therefore, if we know that music can impact some of the very processes that we expect to be impacted through DBT skills training, how does the combination of the two impact DBT skills training outcomes?

To date, there is a dearth of research that has been published in this area. Chwalek and McKinney (2015) interviewed music therapists conducting DBT to understand more about how DBT is perceived by these therapists and how it is being implemented. Results indicated what we already know:

there is a lack of empirical evidence to inform, refine, and guide practice, although components of DBT were valued by those interviewed. I am aware of only two published studies examining the role of music therapy within a DBT program, both of which are published in German by German researchers (Kupski, 2007; Plener *et al.*, 2010). Translations indicate that the studies are in case study form and thus no quasi-experimental or randomized controlled studies exist comparing music therapy DBT to standard DBT to determine if it has an added benefit. Deborah Spiegel and Music Therapy Assistant Professor from The University of Kansas, Abbey Dvorak, PhD, were interested in exploring this gap in the literature further. They conducted a quasi-experimental study with Lindsey Landeck, MT-BC and William Dyer, MS, LLP of Kalamazoo Psychiatric Hospital. They compared participant outcomes from a DBT skills group with a combined DBT skills and music therapy group on attendance, participation, quantity, and frequency of skills practiced as reported on the diary card, and client comprehension of the skills. This study is close to completion and is in the data analysis phase (Dvorak *et al.*).

It is clear that further research including randomized controlled trials is needed in order to determine whether music's addition to DBT improves treatment outcomes on these aforementioned variables. Nonetheless, it is promising to see the early phases of this research, along with the robust base of science that exists about music's impact on the very processes we expect to see impacted by DBT, pointing us in the direction of understanding this area further.

In 2012 Deborah invited me to help train music therapists in DBT and how music therapy interventions could be tailored to the skills acquisition and generalization of DBT skills. Through our online trainings, we have introduced this approach to hundreds of music therapists and have created a more intensive program that includes intensive skills training through Behavioral Tech, webinars on music therapy applied to DBT for each skills training module, personal skills practice and lesson plan writing for each module, and monthly consultation meetings, culminating with an in-depth case report. We wanted to ensure the training was as rigorous as the material requires, taking pride in ensuring that all participants leave the program with a solid understanding of DBT skills, group implementation and management, and the knowledge to apply music therapy interventions to enhance skills acquisition and generalization. This has been a very rewarding part of my career thus far and I have felt very honored to have learned from so many creative-minded and eager-to-learn music therapists. A large part of the inspiration in creating this book has come from the creative ideas and contributions of the participants in this program and we want to say thank you! Without them, this book would still be just an idea and not a reality. In fact, one of the program participants, Suzanne Makary, was invited to be a co-author of this very book because of her particularly creative ideas! Thank you, Suzanne, for being such an active part of the creation process with us.

In Deborah's first, self-published, edition of this book, she presented music therapy interventions to teach many DBT skills, based on Dr. Linehan's first edition of the skills training manual (1994) with the music therapist in mind. For this edition, we wanted to expand the audience who could benefit from incorporating these activities into their work and therefore have included activities that do not require music training nor a certification in music therapy to implement them. We have included many types of music activities with the corresponding DBT skills that are being modeled through the activity, so that these activities can be used flexibly and as desired. It is written in lesson plan form, so it is as user friendly as possible. We have also included a second part of this book with additional activities written in a self-help format that can be handed out as supplements to your clients to practice for homework.

Thank you, Deborah, for carrying the passion for DBT and music therapy so strongly and being such a pioneer in this field. Your trainings and ambition have helped countless music therapists broaden their scope as practitioners, allowing them to further disseminate the power of DBT skills within their skill set as music therapists while aiming to preserve the integrity of the treatment. I am excited to share this book with the world so that DBT can continue to enter the lives of those who could benefit from the knowledge and incorporation of these skills, helping them to create the life worth living that they deserve.

REFERENCES

Chwalek, C. M., & McKinney, C. H. (2015). The use of dialectical behavior therapy (DBT) in music therapy: A sequential explanatory study. *Journal of Music Therapy, 52*(2), 282–318.

Dvorak, A. L., Landeck, L., Dyer, W., & Spiegel, D. (in progress). Comparison of a DBT skills group and a combined DBT skills with music therapy group on client outcomes.

Kupski, G. (2007). Borderline disorder and music therapy in the context of dialectical-behavioral treatment (DBT) [Abstract]. *Musiktherapeutische Umschau, 28*, 17–27.

Lee, J. H. (2016). The effects of music on pain: A meta-analysis. *Journal of Music Therapy, 53*(4), 430–477.

Linehan, M. M. (1994). *Skills Training Manual for Treating Borderline Personality Disorder.* New York, NY: Guilford Press.

Pelletier, C. L. (2004). The effect of music on decreasing arousal due to stress: A meta-analysis. *Journal of Music Therapy, 41*(3), 192–214.

Plener, P., Thorsten, S., Ludolph, A., & Stegemann, T. (2010). "Stop cutting-rock!": A pilot study of a music therapeutic program for self-injuring adolescents. *Music and Medicine, 2*, 59–65.

Thaut, M. H. (2005). *Rhythm, Music, and the Brain: Scientific Foundations and Clinical Applications.* New York, NY: Routledge.

Thaut, M. M., & Hoemberg, V. (2014). *Handbook of Neurologic Music Therapy.* Oxford, UK: Oxford University Press.

INTRODUCTION

WHAT WILL YOU GET OUT OF THIS BOOK?

One thing that prompted the creation of this book was the intention to provide ideas to DBT and other **clinicians** wishing to have some music activities and creative ideas to implement with their existing practices to strengthen what clients are being taught in DBT skills groups. Clinicians, you will get new ideas to use with your clients individually and in groups or to give as homework.

When I first started out as the **music therapist** on a DBT treatment team, I wished there was a how-to book to get me started. This was another motivation for creating this book: to give music therapists and other adjunct therapists the step up that they may need to get started if they're working in a DBT program or for use with clients in their own practice and to spark some new ideas to try or modify. Music therapists, you can even use it as a quick "grab-an-intervention-and-go" book.

I received an email from a more-than-excited DBT clinician who told me she had my book out on the table and a client started reading it. This gave her the idea to ask me to write a version of the book in a **self-help** format. This led to the workbook section of the book (Part 2). Here are ways you can use the workbook section.

- ◆ **Therapists** can provide their clients with handouts so they can do the activities on their own to reinforce or strengthen a skill they learned.

- ◆ **Clinicians** can also use the activities themselves if they need a new idea for a particular skill they are teaching or want something creative and different.

- ◆ **Clients** can use this section on their own as maintenance of their DBT skills after graduating from treatment.

- ◆ **Personal growth seekers** can use this as a self-help section for the acquisition or strengthening of practical life skills.

WHAT TO EXPECT

This is a collection of therapeutic music activities to teach, strengthen, and anchor DBT skills (and other positive life skills).

Part 1 consists of group activities for therapists and group leaders to use. They are modified from the original self-published version of this book (published by Authorhouse in 2010) providing possible DBT skills that each activity could be used to teach or reinforce, and different ways to focus the presentation of the activity to highlight that skill. In this edition, you will be given the main goal, materials needed, and instructions for each group activity. With a different focus, the same activity can also be used to acquire or strengthen a different skill.

In **Part 2**, each DBT skill is presented with its own activity and clear step-by-step instructions. Part 2 presents one activity for each skill in the order they appear in the DBT Skills Training handouts. The material in Part 2 is available to download from www.jkp.com/voucher using the code HUUWAHE.

Some of my original songs are recorded on a CD called *You'll Make It Through the Rain!* and can be downloaded from www.jkp.com/voucher using the code HUUWAHE. Lyrics to the songs can be found within this book. Other songs I have written or other popular songs that are provided as examples in this book are suggested in the text as they relate to a particular activity and DBT skill.

My intent is to provide activities that are my original creations, as well as interventions my students have provided during their training programs, which are used with their permission. I want to thank all those who have contributed in any way to my work, knowingly or unknowingly.

The activities presented are a sample and are meant to help you to generate your own ideas or to remind you of other activities you already know that you can use to strengthen the DBT skills. Feel free to add, subtract, modify, improvise, or change any idea, making sure to preserve the essence of the DBT skill you are aiming to teach and/or strengthen.

INSTRUCTIONS FOR EFFECTIVE RESULTS

It is important to note that there are other texts, such as Linehan's *DBT Skills Training Manual, 2nd edition* (2015) and Rathus and Miller's *DBT Skills Manual for Adolescents* (2015), that give a thorough explanation of the DBT skills, as well as instructions for how to teach these skills in a group format. It is also highly recommended that clinicians complete the DBT skills training class from: behavioraltech.org.

This book provides resources to expand DBT skills teaching in creative, musical ways. When using this book, skills leaders, after doing an activity with group members, are encouraged to tie it together with the featured DBT skill. Ask group members what DBT skills were practiced in the activity they just did or explain to them what skill they practiced and how.

The instructions and activities are written with the non-musician in mind, so those with and without a musical background can use them.

CONTENT NOTE

This book makes mention of self-harm in the context of working with clients and the therapeutic process. Pages 65, 71, 72, 73, and 74 make explicit reference to self-harm. In an outpatient DBT group the clients go home after group, and may not have any support, so it is not advised to talk explicitly about harming yourself or self-harm with clients. The information contained in this book is not intended to replace the services of trained medical professionals or to be a substitute for medical advice. You and/or your clients are advised to consult a doctor on any matters relating to your health, and in particular on any matters that may require diagnosis or medical attention.

MUSIC THERAPY

As defined by the American Music Therapy Association:

> Music therapy is the clinical and evidence-based use of music interventions to accomplish individualized goals within a therapeutic relationship by a credentialed professional who has completed an approved music therapy program.
>
> Music therapy is an established health profession in which music is used…to address physical, emotional, cognitive, and social needs of individuals. After assessing the strengths and needs of each client, the qualified music therapist provides the indicated treatment including creating, singing, moving to, and/or listening to music. Through musical involvement in the therapeutic context, clients' abilities are strengthened and transferred to other areas of their lives. Music therapy also provides avenues for communication that can be helpful to those who find it difficult to express themselves in words.
>
> Research in music therapy supports its effectiveness in many areas such as: overall physical rehabilitation and facilitating movement, increasing people's motivation to become engaged in their treatment, providing emotional support for clients and their families, and providing an outlet for expression of feelings. (American Music Therapy Association, 1998–2019)

A music therapist must adhere to the music therapy professional standards of practice and code of ethics and demonstrate competencies as outlined by the American Music Therapy Association and the Certification Board for Music Therapy. Continuing education and re-certification are required to maintain board certification credentials.

Please note that using the resources in this book cannot be called music therapy unless you are a qualified music therapist. You are free to utilize them as therapeutic activities.

For more information about music therapy, what it takes to be qualified as a music therapist, or to locate a board-certified music therapist, visit: www. musictherapy.org.

DBT SKILLS SUMMARY

Following is a list of DBT skills, summarized from the second edition of the *DBT Skills Training Manual* by Dr. Marsha Linehan (2015) as well as Rathus and Miller's adolescent version (2015). The skills summarized here are highlighted in Part 1 through group activities geared towards the clinician. Part 2 provides a more in-depth look at learning and/or teaching each skill written in a self-help format.

CORE MINDFULNESS SKILLS

- **3 States of Mind**: Emotion Mind, Reasonable Mind, and Wise Mind.

- **What Skills**: Observe, Describe, and Participate.

- **How Skills**: One-Mindfully, Non-Judgmentally, and Effectively.

DISTRESS TOLERANCE SKILLS
Crisis Survival Skills

- **STOP** (Stop, Take a step back, Observe, and Proceed mindfully) for reducing engagement in impulsive behaviors.

- Thinking about **Pros and Cons** to evaluate my behaviour.

- **TIPP** (Temperature, Intense exercise, Paired breathing or Progressive muscle relaxation) to address the body's response to distress.

- Distracting with Wise Mind **ACCEPTS**: Activities, Contributing, Comparisons (or Count your blessings), opposite Emotions, Pushing away, other Thoughts, or Sensations.

- **Self-Soothe**: with vision, hearing, smell, taste, touch, movement.

- **IMPROVE** the Moment with **I**magery, **M**eaning, **P**rayer, **R**elaxation, focus on **O**ne thing in the moment, brief **V**acation, and self-**E**ncouragement.

Reality Acceptance Skills

- **Radical Acceptance** of what is.
- **Turning the mind** again and again.
- Practicing **Willingness** versus **Willfulness**.
- **Half-Smiling**.
- **Willing Hands**.
- **Allowing the mind**: Mindfulness of current thoughts.

EMOTION REGULATION SKILLS
Identifying and Labeling Emotions

- **Observing and Describing emotions** (prompting event, vulnerability factors, thoughts/interpretation, body reaction, urges, body language, facial expressions, actions, emotions, after effects).

Changing Unwanted Emotions

- **Check the Facts**.
- **Problem Solving**.
- **Opposite Action**: changing emotions by acting opposite to the current emotion.

Reducing Vulnerability to Emotion Mind

- **Building Mastery**: doing something a little challenging to make yourself feel more competent and in control.
- **Coping Ahead**.

- Increasing Positive Emotions by **doing pleasant things** that are possible now.

- Building a life worth living by **Accumulating Positives** in the long term.

- PLEASE: taking care of your body (treat PhysicaL illness, balance Eating, avoid mood-Altering drugs, balance Sleep, Exercise).

INTERPERSONAL EFFECTIVENESS SKILLS

- Using **DEAR MAN** to get what you want or say no when your objective is the most important priority: Describe, Express, Assert, Reinforce, stay Mindful, Appear confident, Negotiate.

- Using **GIVE** when relationship is most important: be Gentle, act Interested, Validate, and use an Easy manner.

- Using **FAST** when self-respect is most important: be Fair, no Apologies, Stick to your values, be Truthful.

- Considering the factors in asking and saying no, and using the appropriate intensity level.

WALKING THE MIDDLE PATH

- Use **Dialectics** to observe the truth in multiple perspectives and to reduce polarization with others.

- **Validate** others as well as yourself.

- Increase desired behaviors or decrease ineffective habits through **Behaviorism**.

Part 1

GROUP ACTIVITIES FOR CLINICIANS TO FACILITATE

LISTENING TO MUSIC

❀ CHOOSE A SONG THAT DESCRIBES YOU
Main Goal

This music-listening activity asks group members to pick a piece of music that describes them, creating an opportunity for self-disclosure and group rapport building. Each piece of music may affect each group member differently based on their interpretations of and associated memories with the song, providing many opportunities for group discussion and skills reinforcement.

Step 5 in the instructions allows for review of DBT skills as these discussion questions are answered, and it can serve as a tool to assess skills comprehension.

DBT Skills that Are Strengthened

When you present this activity, modify your approach based on which skill you are highlighting.

Core mindfulness: Listen One-Mindfully to the song that is selected, focusing on the lyrics, and practice being Non-Judgmental of other people's selections.

Emotion regulation: Observe and Describe your current emotions as you listen to each song and/or as you select your song.

Distress tolerance: Practice distracting with Wise Mind ACCEPTS by engaging in the group activity.

Supplies Needed

- A list of songs that the group members can select from and listen to.

- Some means of playing and listening to the songs (such as CDs, MP3s, computer, iPad, phone, or other technology).

Instructions

1. Ask group participants to choose a song that describes something about themselves. Instruct the group not to base their choice solely on liking the singer or the sound of the song but rather to select a song based on whether they feel the lyrics resonate with something about themselves that they would be willing to share with the group.

2. Ask for a volunteer or choose a group member to start. Play the song that they chose. Ask everyone to listen to the selected song and to be prepared to share what their experience was like (i.e., their thoughts and interpretation of the song, emotions, sensations, urges) while listening to the song.

3. After listening to their song, have the person who chose it describe why they chose that song.

4. Ask the other group members what their observations were while listening to the song.

5. If time allows, ask group members other questions such as the following.

   - What skills would you recommend the person in the song use?

   - Were there any skills used in the song?

   - What skills could group members use or have they used when faced with similar situations?

6. Repeat until each group member has shared their song with the group.

Examples

Perfect by Simple Plan, "because I'm not perfect enough so Dad left me."

Skills the group members suggested for the person who shared this song: Check the Facts regarding interpretation (or misinterpretation) of events that prompted these emotions and determine if emotions are justified or unjustified, Self-Soothe, IMPROVE the Moment with self-encouragement.

One Step Closer by Linkin Park, "because I feel one step closer to the edge of angry outbursts."

Skills the group members suggested for the person who shared this song: Self-Soothe, Imagery, Breathing, Pros and Cons.

Good Riddance (Time of Your Life) by Green Day, "because I want to get through this part of my life and look back and say I had a good life, made good decisions, and got through it and had a good life."

Skills the group members suggested for the person who shared this song: Increase positive emotions with goal-setting.

Blue by Eiffel 65, "because this is how I feel."

Skills the group members suggested for the person who shared this song: Self-Soothe, increase positive emotions.

✿ THOUGHTS AND FEELINGS
Main Goal

This is an exercise to increase self-expression, self-awareness, and emotional release, and to give an opportunity to review, reinforce, and actively practice skills.

DBT Skills that Are Strengthened

When you present this activity, modify your approach based on which skill you are highlighting.

Core mindfulness: This activity can reinforce the What Skills of Observing and Describing through words or art and Participating through the task. It also can strengthen the How Skills by encouraging clients to listen and write or draw One-Mindfully, Non-Judgmentally, and Effectively.

Emotion regulation: In making connections to their emotions as they listen and then express, participants are practicing Understanding and Naming emotions, ways to Describe emotions, and possibly Accumulating Positive Emotions.

Distress tolerance: As the participants engage, they can be practicing distress tolerance skills such as: distract with Wise Mind ACCEPTS (Activities, Contributing, Comparisons, Thoughts, Sensations), Self-Soothe, Willingness, IMPROVE the Moment.

Supplies Needed

- ◆ Recorded music to play.

- ◆ Paper, pencils, markers, colors, art supplies, etc.

Instructions

1. Choose several songs to play. Try to vary the styles of music. Have group members listen to the music and, while listening, write down their feelings and thoughts about each song or even draw to the music.

2. Follow by sharing and discussion of skills.

Examples

Hope by Shaggy: "If I didn't have hope when I roll out of bed each morning, I would probably be dead. Never forget that there is always hope."

With Arms Wide Open by Creed: "This song made me feel hopeful and think about showing my baby the world."

Oops!... I Did It Again by Britney Spears: "So many times I've messed up. I need to realize that I'm not only hurting myself but others, and it hurts to know I'm causing that pain. I've made too many people believe that I'm getting better when, in fact, I'm slowly dying away inside."

Wishing It Was by Santana: "This song makes me feel good. I can relate to it because I always wish things were different. But I am hopeful, and I know things will change and be better."

Kryptonite by 3 Doors Down: "This song is about me and the secrets I keep about my dad."

✿ LYRIC ANALYSIS
Main Goal

Lyric analysis involves listening to music with a focus on discussing something about the lyrics afterward. It can be used for focusing and for self-expression, self-exploration, and self-disclosure. Also, since there is a plethora of choices of songs that have lyrics that can be interpreted to be meaningful in some way, it allows for opportunities to reinforce so many of the DBT skills, as you will see listed below.

DBT Skills that Are Strengthened

When you present this activity, modify your approach based on which skill you are highlighting.

Core mindfulness: If your focus is on core mindfulness, this activity emphasizes What and How Skills as participants listen to and analyze the lyrics. You could practice Wise Mind by asking half the group to listen for facts and the other half to listen for emotions to teach the states of mind (e.g., *Say* by John Mayer).

Emotion regulation: Identify and Describe emotion by asking what emotion you imagine the singer was feeling and why (e.g., *I Don't Care Anymore* by Phil Collins), Check the Facts by exploring if the emotion is justified by the lyrics (e.g., *Before He Cheats* by Carrie Underwood), Accumulate Positive Emotions by exploring coping techniques that the artist may or may not express in the lyrics (e.g., *My Favorite Things* from The Sound of Music). Listen to the song with a focus on exploring values (e.g., *Some Nights* by Fun). Use Opposite Action by listening to *The Lazy Song* by Bruno Mars and use prompts to explore action urge to sadness versus its Opposite Action.

Distress tolerance: Listening to the lyrics of the song can be an act of distraction (with Activities). Any call-to-action song could demonstrate Contributing, such as anti-war songs. Listen to the lyrics of a song such as *Rehab* by Amy Winehouse and practice Comparisons through identifying clients' struggles versus singers' struggles and the fact that the client is learning these skills. Focusing on the lyrics could be an example of the skill of distracting with other Thoughts.

Radical Acceptance can be explored by listening to song lyrics such as *Let It Be* by The Beatles or *Meant to Be* by Florida Georgia Line and Bebe Rexha. Focusing on the lyrics of a song such as *Take It Easy* by the Eagles can highlight the Self-Soothe skill. IMPROVE the Moment with Imagery can be practiced by focusing on the images the lyrics evoke (e.g., *Feelin' Groovy* by Simon and Garfunkel). Discussing what the lyrics mean to each person is practicing Meaning. If they are participating, they are practicing One Thing in the Moment. The use of *Toes* by Zac Brown Band is an example of lyrics highlighting the skill of vacation.

Interpersonal effectiveness: Listen to lyrics and decide if the singer used DEAR MAN to ask for what they want or how they could reword it using the skill. Explore whether the singer is using GIVE to keep the relationship and/ or FAST to reinforce self-respect. *Before He Cheats* by Carrie Underwood is an example of a song where the singer is not using the GIVE skill. *King of Anything* by Sara Bareilles can highlight the FAST skill. *If I Only Had the Words (to Tell You)* by Billy Joel can prompt discussion related to DEAR MAN.

Supplies Needed

- A print out of a song's lyrics and a recording of the song. You can use just about any song, keeping in mind what is appropriate to listen to with your group members.

- Paper, pencils, markers, colors, art supplies, etc.

Instructions

1. Pass out a copy of the lyrics first, if possible.

2. Decide which skill you're highlighting, orient group members to the skill, and provide directions for what should be focused on as they listen to the lyrics.

3. Ask thought provoking questions that pertain to the skill that you are highlighting through the lyric analysis.

4. Another option is to print out questions and have group members answer the questions as they listen and then share.

5. Group members may also be prompted to highlight a line of the lyrics that is meaningful to them to discuss.

✤ NAME THAT TUNE/SING THE NEXT LINE
Main Goal

This musical game involves working together to practice and reinforce skills while building pleasant experiences.

DBT Skills that Are Strengthened

Core mindfulness: During this game, participants will be listening One-Mindfully, and through engaging fully in the present moment they will be using the What Skill of Participate.

Emotion regulation: If they enjoy the game, they could be practicing Accumulating Positives by participating in the game.

Distress tolerance: If they are in distress, participating in the game could be using the distract skill with Wise Mind ACCEPTS (Activities).

Supplies Needed

- A variety of recorded songs.
- Paper or a white board to keep score.

Instructions

1. Divide the group into teams.

2. Play a song. The first team has 30 seconds to name that tune, and when you stop the music, someone from that team has to sing the next line.

3. After you stop the music and someone sings the next line, play the music again to see if they were correct.

4. Award two points for naming the tune and another two points for singing the next line correctly.

5. If the first team doesn't guess correctly in time, the second team can try to guess the same song after listening for the next 30 seconds.

6. Play the next song and let the second team guess the song. If the second team doesn't guess correctly in time, the first team gets to try.

✿ BINGO
Main Goal

This game utilizes mindfully paying attention while using familiar songs to practice skills while building pleasant experiences.

DBT Skills that Are Strengthened

Core mindfulness: During this game, participants will be listening One-Mindfully, and by engaging fully in the present moment they will be using the What Skill of Participate.

Emotion regulation: If they enjoy the game, they could be practicing Accumulating Positives by participating in the game.

Distress tolerance: If they are in distress, participating in the game could be using the distract skill with Wise Mind ACCEPTS (Activities).

Supplies Needed

- On the next page is a blank bingo game form. Fill in the blanks with song titles that are familiar to the group members. Rearrange the sequence on each bingo card so no one gets bingo at the same time.

- Bring recordings of each of the songs.

Instructions

1. Play each song for 30 seconds. Players put a marker on their bingo card on the corresponding song title. Anyone who knows the answer says the answer out loud so that everyone else knows which one to mark.

2. Whoever gets bingo (the first player to have a marker on five spots in a row horizontally, diagonally, or vertically across the page) has to read off the titles in the winning row to verify that all the songs were played. They then get to choose a song to listen to, and the entire song is played.

3. Another way to play is to give a verbal cue such as, "This song was the theme song to a Disney movie," and the group members look on the card and guess *The Lion Sleeps Tonight*. Whoever guesses correctly first gets to give the next clue. The person giving clues cannot use the title as part of the clue.

B I N G O

SONG WRITING

✿ POSITIVE AFFIRMATIONS
Main Goal

Song writing encourages self-reflection. How and what we say to ourselves can be expressed creatively as we work towards building positive emotions and thoughts.

DBT Skills that Are Strengthened

When you present this activity, modify your approach based on which skill you are highlighting.

Core mindfulness: The How Skill of "Non-Judgmentally" is emphasized in this song-writing activity.

Emotion regulation: Writing affirmations can be used to Accumulate Positive Emotions in the short term. Self-reflection may necessitate the use of Check the Facts.

Distress tolerance: This particular song-writing activity can also be an example of the skill "Encouragement" from IMPROVE the Moment.

About Affirmations

An affirmation is a positive statement, in the present tense, as if it is happening now.

The problem with negative thoughts is that they can become self-fulfilling prophecies. We talk ourselves into believing that we're not good enough. And, as a result, these thoughts drag down our personal lives, our relationships, and our careers.

But, if we deliberately use positive thoughts about ourselves, the effect can be just as powerful but far more helpful. (Hence an affirmation.)

When you repeat the positive affirmations often, and believe in them, you can start to make positive changes. (Mind Tools 1996–2019)

Music is a powerful way to anchor thoughts into our mind. TV ads and radio commercials use jingles that stay in our heads, often leading people to buy whatever is being advertised. What better way to reprogram our mind with positive affirmations and words of encouragement than to write a song and put the positive lyrics to music?!

Thoughts can either limit us or help us create the results we want. The idea is to become aware of our thoughts and to allow only positive thoughts to dominate our thinking. We will be painting a picture of what we want to be true as if it already is. By telling ourselves we can succeed, we can.

Supplies Needed

- Paper, pencils.

- Karaoke music if you have some and want to use it.

Instructions

1. Have group members fill in these blanks: I deserve _____, I am willing to _____, I am learning to _____.

2. Ask them to share what they have written.

3. Ask them how it felt to say the statements (e.g., positive, encouraging, empowering).

4. Ask group members to write out three negative things they tell themselves: I am _____ _____. Ask them to turn these into positive affirmations. For example: "I always make mistakes. I am stupid. I never do anything right." Affirmation: "I am getting better every time I do this. I am learning every day. It's okay to make mistakes. Willingness to fail leads to success." Note: Make sure you prompt the group members to use the skill of Check the Facts if they are having a hard time wording their affirmation in a non-judgmental way.

5. Give the following direction: "Paint a picture in words of how you want things to be for you. You can use the sentences with the filled in

blanks if you want. This can look like a song, a rap, a paragraph, some sentences describing what you put in those three blanks or using other affirmations." You could arrange this as a partner activity.

6. You can offer the use of karaoke CDs for background music when they read or rap their story, poem, or song. They can choose to sing their song without music or may just read it.

Group Members' Song Examples Using Affirmations

I can get through this because I know I can do anything I put my mind to
I'm good at what I do and I can accomplish whatever I try to
I'm smart and loveable, have faith in myself
I am great, strong, unique unlike anyone else
I work hard learn DBT using skills every day
I handle depression and avoid aggression or oppression, cope well with
    words I can't say
I'm free, my life is good, I let others in
Communicate, be a success, just got to begin

I can do it I know that I can
I can go any length, with you by my side
I can feel it now, so sure and so true
I'm gonna make it, and to my heart be true

I strive
I'm determined
Learning the ropes to achieve
I strive
I'm determined
So give me my papers I'm ready to
    leave

Because I'm awake and aware now
Determined to succeed
Because I'm awake and aware now
Determined to succeed

I can survive
Stay off the dope
I have
A life
I'm learning now how to really cope

Because I'm awake and aware now
Determined to succeed
Because I'm awake and aware now
Determined to succeed

I am
Motivated
Exercise makes me elated
I take
My medications
So I don't get agitated

Because I'm awake and aware now
Determined to succeed
Because I'm awake and aware now
Determined to succeed

If I
Stay away
From drug abuse
I won't go
Waka doodle
Or knock a screw loose

Because I'm awake and aware now
Determined to succeed
Because I'm awake and aware now
Determined to succeed

To work
Is to live
To live is to be free
The sweet
Sweet freedom
of sobriety

Because I'm awake and aware now
Determined to succeed
Because I'm awake and aware now
Determined to succeed

✾ METAPHORS
Main Goal
Explore aspects of self through imagery and action words, sharing with others, and creative self-expression.

DBT Skills that Are Strengthened
When you present this activity, modify your approach based on which skill you are highlighting.

Core mindfulness: The What Skills of Observe and Describe are practiced through self-reflection. Non-Judgmentalness is practiced while group members describe themselves and their lives.

Emotion regulation: The instructions focus on having group members identify and label emotions and Practice Mindfulness of current emotions.

Distress tolerance: Writing about their reality as it is can be an effective way to practice Radical Acceptance. Willingness is needed to experience emotions that arise during this activity.

Supplies Needed
* A list of action words (such as slide, glide, blow, flow, jump, fall) and/or metaphors (such as a sinking ship, a maze, a castle) that group members can use to describe themselves and/or their lives.

Instructions
1. Pass out the list of action words and/or metaphors and have each person circle any of the words that describe them or that resonate with them. Ask group members to be mindful of any emotions they experience during this activity and to practice Willingness to experience these emotions.

2. Ask them to write sentences describing why they circled those words.

3. Write a song, rap, poem, or paragraph from their sentences and words.

4. Help group members process their songs to identify where there may be judgments, non-dialectical thinking, or hopelessness present. Validate the valid!

Group Members' Song Examples Using Metaphors

"My life reminds me of two different things: a maze and a lonely crowd. A maze because my life takes many turns; sometimes I find a deer path and sometimes I run into a wall. A lonely crowd because very few people understand what's going on to talk with me yet there are hundreds of people around."

I'm in a maze
Can't find my way out
I turn and turn
I look about
I do not know

From where I came
But surely know
I've got me to blame...

My life is like a battlefield
Because every day I live is
A fight to go on
Nobody feels what I feel
So I bite my tongue
And move on

My life is like a lonely crowd
Waiting to be heard
Wanting to be loved and
    understood
Not knowing or realizing
No one really cares

My life is like thin ice
For I never know
How long it will be
Before I fall in to all
The hurt and pain I feel

⚘ GROUP SONG WRITING

Main Goal

The goal of this group experience is for group members to work together, to each contribute to the group process, to express themselves, to brainstorm, to be heard, to be unique, and to be creative while practicing skills.

DBT Skills that Are Strengthened

When you present this activity, modify your approach based on which skill you are highlighting.

Core mindfulness: Working together allows for practice of the How Skills of Non-Judgmental and Effective.

Emotion regulation: Taking the steps to create a song from start to finish can help to Build Mastery and may also be experienced as a pleasant activity (Accumulating Positives).

Distress tolerance: Writing and sharing in this group song may bring opportunities to use Radical Acceptance and Willingness, especially if one does not like another person's contributions.

Interpersonal effectiveness: Through this team activity, practicing GIVE towards one's peers is important, as well as contributing your own thoughts by adding FAST.

Supplies Needed

- ◆ White board and markers.
- ◆ Paper and pencil.

Instructions

1. Choose a topic to write the song about. You may come prepared with examples of song topics if the group members are unsure of what they would like to have as the song's theme.

2. Ask each person to tell you a line about that topic. Write the lines up on the white board, not necessarily in the final order. Write exactly what they say as an opportunity to be validating.

3. Now focus on editing. Move the lines into the order that the group thinks makes sense. You can change endings to rhyme if desired. The process can either flow organically or the group leader can facilitate a lot of the editing.

4. Ask someone to sing the first line. Ask someone else to sing the next line and so on. The group leader or a group member can play guitar chords to give it structure. Or you can leave out this step and just have the song to read or rap.

Song Example

This song was written in a group using the method described above. The topic was DBT. Each group member said a line—one after the other. In this case the lines fit pretty much in the order they were given.

DBT's the way I start my day
It helps me out in every single way
Like a broken record it plays in my head
To use my Wise Mind instead
Playing over and over when my mood sways
I have lots of wonderful days
Pros and Cons, Wise Mind, just to name a few
I like using these; you should try them, too
Sadness, anger, misery are all helped effectively with DBT
It's an awesome part of my every day
Tomorrow, forever, and the next day
It helps me always; it's good skills to know
DBT rocks—Hooray! Hooray!

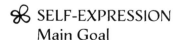 SELF-EXPRESSION
Main Goal

This activity is song writing for self-expression, creativity, and an opportunity to review, strengthen, and actively practice skills.

DBT Skills that Are Strengthened

When you present this activity, modify your approach based on which skill you are highlighting.

Core mindfulness: What Skills of Observe, Describe, and Participate can be explored through writing about and connecting to the DBT skill; How Skills can be practiced as group members write, through being Non-Judgmental of themselves, working with Effectiveness, and being One-Mindful.

Emotion regulation: Writing the song demonstrates Building Mastery by being able to speak to the skill. Completing the task Accumulates Positives through creative writing.

Distress tolerance: Writing about the skill incorporates distraction through ACCEPTS (Activities, Contributing, Thoughts). IMPROVE the Moment may be incorporated in their writing with the use of Imagery, finding Meaning, or a brief Vacation. They will be practicing focusing on One Thing in the Moment and self-Encouragement.

This exercise can be used to reinforce just about any skill depending on what skill they choose to, or you suggest they, write about.

Supplies Needed

- Paper and pencils.

Instructions

1. Ask group members to choose a song they know and like.

2. Pass out paper and pencils and have group members write their own lyrics to that song on the topic of a DBT skill—either a skill of their choice or one you assign.

3. Share.

Example of Writing New Lyrics to an Existing Song

(Holiday song to the tune of Jingle Bells)

The holidays are near
It's almost Christmas Day
We're learning DBT
Use skills every day

We can make it through
Filled with lots of hope
Avoiding aggression
With skills that help us cope

We'll have a big party
Our urges might be strong
We want to get to go to it
We're using Pros and Cons

Thinking positive
Letting go of stress
Learning to communicate
and be a great success

DBT, DBT, DBT all day
Self-Soothe, Distraction, Willingness
DEAR MAN to get our way
DBT, DBT, DBT's okay
It keeps us cool so we use Wise Mind
It's such a better way

DBT, DBT, DBT all day
Self-Soothe, Distraction, Willingness
DEAR MAN to get our way
DBT, DBT, DBT's okay
It keeps us cool so we use Wise Mind
It's such a better way

MOVEMENT

PASS THE MOVE

Main Goal

This activity encourages creativity, self-expression, mindful awareness, memory, and just plain fun to get a group moving! It's also a good way to learn people's names if you ask them to say their name when it's their turn and you say it every time you do their movement.

DBT Skills that Are Strengthened

When you present this activity, modify your approach based on which skill you are highlighting.

Core mindfulness: What Skills of Observe, Describe, and Participate are practiced through movement and mindful awareness of the beat. By keeping track of who the current leader is and what the leader is doing, the How Skills are developed through Non-Judgmentally engaging and being One-Mindful and Effective.

Distress tolerance: While participating in the movements, members can be practicing distracting with ACCEPTS (Activities, Thoughts), and practicing Willingness through taking a healthy risk.

Emotion regulation: As the choreography develops and through the repeated practice, Building Mastery is accomplished. Moving to the beat Accumulates Positive Emotions. Taking a healthy risk to lead a movement can emphasize the value of Opposite Action.

Supplies Needed

- Recorded music with a good dance beat.

Instructions

1. Stand in a circle and play the music. One person leads the group in a simple movement that everyone does together for eight beats of the music.

2. The second person does their movement, which everyone copies for the same number of beats.

3. Go back to the first movement, then the second, and then add a third movement.

4. Start from the beginning each time, adding each new movement as you move around the circle until everyone has been added into the choreography one at a time. Go around the entire circle.

✿ MIRRORING

Main Goal

This activity encourages self-expression, mindful awareness, focus, and allowing the self to connect to another through moving to the music. It also allows people to move beyond self-imposed limitations or fears by taking the opportunity to practice Opposite Action.

DBT Skills that Are Strengthened

When you present this activity, modify your approach based on which skill you are highlighting.

Core mindfulness: What Skills of Observe, Describe, and Participate are practiced through movement and mindful awareness of the beat and the partner. How Skills are developed through Non-Judgmentally engaging and being One-Mindful and Effective.

Distress tolerance: While participating in the movements, members can be practicing distracting with ACCEPTS (Activities, Thoughts) and practicing Willingness through taking a healthy risk.

Emotion regulation: Moving to the beat can Accumulate Positive Emotions. Taking a healthy risk in being the leader of the pair and moving for the partner to copy can emphasize the value of Opposite Action in a reluctant leader.

Interpersonal effectiveness: If your focus is on these skills, the exercise can encourage expression of needs both verbally and non-verbally, tapping into DEAR MAN when they share what they can and cannot do in Step 3 of the instructions. Validation is experienced through focusing on the partner and attentively mirroring their moves—GIVE.

Supplies Needed

- Recorded music or live music with a beat conducive to stretching (e.g., *I Said... You Said* by Jim Brickman).

Instructions

1. You, the group leader, should partner with someone in the group to demonstrate. Ask your partner to mirror your movements. Then switch so you mirror his/her movements.

2. Ask the group members to choose a partner and stand face to face with adequate room.

3. Ask the group members to share with one another any movements that would be uncomfortable for them (e.g., if someone cannot bend forward or raise an arm due to injury).

4. Ask the pairs to select a leader and a follower (letting them know that they will switch halfway through). Now ask them not to talk but to move to the music and follow their leader. Start the music, and ask them to switch halfway through.

5. At the end of the piece, discuss connection to the skills as well as successes and challenges.

MAKING MUSIC

ACTIVITIES FOR MELODIC INSTRUMENTS

Main Goal

Playing an instrument takes focus, generates feelings of pride, and builds self-esteem. It can distract group members from their problems by helping them focus on the here and now of the music playing. They build mastery by practicing their musical parts over and over until they learn them. Even if group members don't know how to play a musical instrument, they can be set up for success.

DBT Skills that Are Strengthened

When you present this activity, modify your approach based on which skill you are highlighting.

Core mindfulness: Playing an instrument takes focus. If using the option to play as a group, the participants, with a variety of ability levels, engage in the What Skills of Observe, Describe, and Participate. These are practiced through paying attention and knowing when it's their turn. They practice being free of judgment of themselves and others—the How Skills of being Non-Judgmental, Effective, and One-Mindful.

Distress tolerance: Playing an instrument can be a distraction with ACCEPTS (Activities, Contributing, Thoughts). It can provide an experience that is Self-Soothing. It encourages the use of IMPROVE with One Thing in the Moment. Pros and Cons can be explored if they have any disruptive urges, and they could practice Willingness in taking a healthy risk.

Emotion regulation: Accomplishing this challenge demonstrates Building Mastery by learning a new piece to perform. The reluctant performer can experience the use of Opposite Action. Accumulating Positive Emotions can happen through performance.

Interpersonal effectiveness: Decrease isolation and loneliness by participating in the group activity. Practice Mindfulness of others. Participate with others. Become part of the group experience through music making. Working together builds Relationship Effectiveness—GIVE. Music making allows for the practice of Validation within the group.

Supplies Needed

+ Musical instruments such as keyboards, chimes, guitars, violins, xylophones, a QChord, a mandolin, a steel drum, and so forth. The pieces are always shared at the end.

Instructions

1. Label the keys (or whatever makes the notes) with letters representing the note names.

2. Write out a familiar song or songs using the letters of the note names (see the sample song sheet on the next page).

3. This could alternatively be done with colors by assigning a color to each note. Colored dots from an office supply store work well.

4. Depending on the instruments that are selected, the members may choose to create music together or individually. For an individual performance, give each group member an instrument and a song sheet and ask them to choose a song or make up an original tune to play for the group by the end of the hour. They should each focus on their own activity. It will be noisy, so be prepared—instruments with headphones are helpful. Walk around and encourage individuals. After a short time, ask group members to stop and play what they are working on one at a time. You will be impressed.

5. As an alternative, for a group performance that doesn't take much time to rehearse, divide a song into sections and give each participant a section. For example, *The Twelve Days of Christmas* can be divided like this:

    ▪ Person 1 has the melody for "On the X day of Christmas, my true love gave to me."

    ▪ Person 2 has the melody for "a partridge in a pear tree."

- Person 3 has the melody for "Two turtle doves."

- And so on, with each person taking turns playing their line on cue.

   Another group idea is to assign each group member a letter name. Put the notes of a song on the board and point to the notes one at a time in rhythm and in order of the song.

Amazing Grace
DG BB AG ED
DG BB AD
BD BG DE ED
DG BB AG

Mary Had a Little Lamb
E D C D E E E DDD EEE
E D C D E E E D D E D C

America (My Country 'tis of Thee)
C C D B CD E E F E DC D C B C
G G G G FE F F F F ED E FEDC E FG
AF E D C

Happy Birthday
GG A G C B
GG A G D C
G G G E C B A
FF E C D C

The Lion Sleeps Tonight
C DE D EF ED C DE D C E D
G ED E GF ED C DE D C E D

❀ ACTIVITIES FOR DRUMS AND RHYTHM INSTRUMENTS
Main Goal

It takes mindfulness to play your own rhythm while someone else is playing theirs. It also takes willingness and impulse control to not just beat the drum incessantly but to take turns. This is a forum for self-expression and practicing building relationships with others.

DBT Skills that Are Strengthened

When you present this activity, modify your approach based on which skill you are highlighting. This activity encourages review of all the skills.

Core mindfulness: Playing an instrument takes focus. The participants, with a variety of ability levels, engage in the What Skills of Observe, Describe, and Participate. These are practiced through paying attention. They practice being free of judgment of themselves and others—the How Skills of being Non-Judgmental, One-Mindful, and Effective.

Emotion regulation: Playing rhythms demonstrates Building Mastery by learning and accumulates positive emotions by making sound.

Distress tolerance: Playing an instrument can be a distraction with ACCEPTS (Activities, Contributing, Thoughts). It can provide an experience that is Self-Soothing. It encourages the use of IMPROVE with One Thing in the Moment. In the application focused on affirmation (option 3) it reinforces Encouragement. Pros and Cons can be explored if they have any disruptive urges, and they could practice Willingness in taking a healthy risk.

Interpersonal effectiveness: Decrease isolation and loneliness by participating in the group activity. This promotes mindfulness of others as members have a shared experience. Music making allows for the practice of Validation within the group. Working together builds Relationship Effectiveness—GIVE.

Supplies Needed

- Drums such as nesting drums, sound shapes, or paddle drums, and a variety of rhythm instruments such as woodblocks, claves, maracas, tambourines, etc. You can also make rhythm instruments out of coffee cans or five-gallon water containers for drums and toilet paper rolls filled with beans for shakers.

Instructions

Choose one of the four activities.

1. Ask group members to name some DBT skills (such as Wise Mind ACCEPTS, Pros and Cons, DEAR MAN, Willingness). Clap the names of the skills.

   - Pass out rhythm instruments and drums.

   - Play the rhythms of the skill names together as a group. For example, say "Wise Mind ACCEPTS," then echo on the instruments several times. Take turns leading, having each group member state a skill name and the group echoing the rhythm of it on their instruments.

   - Divide into groups and assign a different rhythm to each group. It takes mindfulness to focus on your own rhythm. For example, group 1 plays "Pros and Cons (rest)" and group 2 plays "Wise Mind ACCEPTS (rest)" starting on "Cons" so "Cons" and "Wise" happen together. Note: The word "rest" is not spoken; it is a silent beat.

2. Another way to drum using DBT skills is to have someone start and keep a steady beat and ask the group members to mindfully listen while they play their own rhythm. Their task is to create balance between sound and silence. Allow them to improvise and to play whatever they feel like playing on their instrument but ask them to listen for the silence in between the sounds. Say, "If it doesn't sound good, stop and listen, then start again." Have one group of instruments play while the others listen, taking turns, for example, just the wooden instruments, just the shaken instruments, or just the drums. This takes impulse control. Then go back to everyone playing together. Pair people up and have them play together as partners without communicating about it in words. Ask them to just make it sound good by listening mindfully.

3. Another option is for group members to make up a rap to use for DBT rhythms. Here is a DBT rhythm for Pros and Cons. Note: The word "rest" is not spoken; it is a silent beat.

Pros and Cons
Pros and Cons

Think about the consequences when I feel my urges
Think about the consequences when I feel my urges

Stop (rest) and think
Stop (rest) and think

For further instructions on using this song, see the "Songs" section of this book (p.67). It is also one of the songs on the *You'll Make It Through the Rain!* CD and can be downloaded from www.jkp.com/voucher using the code HUUWAHE.

4. A fourth way to use drums and percussion instruments is to generate affirmations, positive words of encouragement such as, "I can do it, I know that I can," and play the rhythm of that on the drum. Take turns around the circle.

❀ RHYTHM ACTIVITY WITH NO INSTRUMENTS
Main Goal
This activity requires mindfulness, paying attention, and focus. It is an activity that can challenge one's self and others while distracting from whatever is happening with us emotionally.

DBT Skills that Are Strengthened
When you present this activity, modify your approach based on which skill you are highlighting.

Core mindfulness: This is definitely a mindfulness challenge. It incorporates the What Skills of Observe, Describe, and Participate and the How Skills of being Non-Judgmental, One-Mindful, and Effective through paying attention, engaging with one's turn, and focusing on the rhythm.

Distress tolerance: This activity uses distraction with ACCEPTS (Activities, Contributing, Thoughts). It encourages the use of IMPROVE with One Thing in the Moment. Pros and Cons can be explored if group members have any disruptive urges, and they could practice Willingness in taking a healthy risk. When a person makes a mistake, misses their turn, or gets "out" they can practice Radical Acceptance.

Emotion regulation: Accomplishing this challenge demonstrates Building Mastery by learning the pattern and Accumulates Positive Emotions through success.

Interpersonal effectiveness: The activity decreases isolation and loneliness through participation in the group activity. Group members can practice mindfulness of others while participating with others.

Instructions

1. Count off so that each person around the circle has a number.
2. Keep a steady quarter note rhythm using your body: hands on knees twice, clap hands together twice, and snap fingers once on each hand.
3. Explain that the first person calls their own number on the first snap and then calls the number of the next person in the circle on the second snap.
4. Go in order until everyone understands: person number one calls out "one, two," person number two calls out "two, three," and so on for however many there are in the circle.
5. Once they have gone around the circle and have done it correctly, instruct group members to call their own number on the first snap and any other person's number on the second snap (e.g "one, six," "six, five," "five, eight"). The person whose number is called on the second snap takes the next turn.
6. Once everyone has mastered it, anyone who hesitates or makes a mistake is out.
7. This can be varied by using people's names.

SINGING KARAOKE

Main Goal

Karaoke is an easy, fairly inexpensive way for a group to have a singalong where all are involved. It's nice that the lyrics can be viewed on the TV screen for all to see. This activity fosters self-expression, group cohesion, and fun.

DBT Skills that Are Strengthened

When you present this activity, modify your approach based on which skill you are highlighting.

Core mindfulness: Whether the singer or listener, this activity incorporates the What Skills of Observe, Describe, and Participate and the How Skills of being Non-Judgmental, One-Mindful, and Effective through paying attention, practicing being free of judging, and participating through singing.

Distress tolerance: This activity uses distraction with ACCEPTS (Activities, Contributing, Thoughts). It encourages the use of IMPROVE with One Thing in the Moment. Pros and Cons can be explored if group members have any disruptive urges, and they could practice Willingness in taking a healthy risk.

Emotion regulation: Getting up the courage to sing in front of a group could take Opposite Action. Accumulating Positive Emotions through doing something in the moment can lead to a pleasant experience.

Interpersonal effectiveness: Decrease isolation and loneliness by participating in the group activity. Practice mindfulness of others. Singing together and/or listening to others sing allows for the practice of Validation within the group.

Supplies Needed

- A karaoke machine and karaoke CDs.

- Microphone.

- Booklet of available songs that group members can select a song from.

Instructions

1. Set up some karaoke rules: respect each other; don't laugh at the singer or make fun of the song that was selected; don't talk during the song; practice being Non-Judgmental.

2. Each person will get a chance to select a song. When it's someone's turn that person can decide whether they want to sing alone on the microphone or sing all together as a group.

GUIDED IMAGERY

�֍ GUIDED IMAGERY

There are several goals for using imagery with individuals and groups. As you can see in the table below, the skills strengthened may depend on the purpose of the imagery. This section includes guides that were written for the goals listed below.

Three goals for using imagery	DBT skills strengthened
1. Relaxation and stress relief	Distress tolerance: Imagery, Breathing
2. Connecting with the Wise Mind	Core mindfulness: Wise Mind
3. Rehearsal/practicing being successful/ Coping Ahead: "What you conceive and believe you can achieve"	Emotion regulation: Building Mastery, Accumulating Positives, Coping Ahead

Instructions

When you present this activity, modify your approach based on which script and goal you are highlighting.

I call my imagery group "Inner Harmony." Prior to using the imagery scripts in the following activities, introduce the group to the experience through the instructions below.

1. Ask group members to define the word harmony. "Peace" is the basic answer. In music, it's when the notes blend well and the sounds complement one another. The way I see it, how can there be peace in the world if there isn't peace within myself first?

2. Tell group members that in this group they will learn a skill that may help them experience inner harmony and that they can use on their own if it works for them.

3. Talk about the power of imagery.

   - A prisoner of war was in solitary confinement for five years. During that time, he practiced his golf swing and imagined winning the world golf championship. When he was released, guess what happened? He won the golf championship.

   - There were two basketball teams; one team practiced shooting hoops every night on the courts while the other just imagined shooting hoops and making the baskets. Who do you think won when they played each other? The team that imagined shooting hoops.

4. Say to the group: "What we conceive and believe, we can achieve. Think about what you want to create for yourself, and we will practice it." Engage in the imagery. After each script encourage the sharing of outcomes through follow-up questions.

❄ RELAXATION AND STRESS RELIEF

Begin by asking the group members: "On a scale of 1–100 how stressed do you feel right now?"

Music

Use relaxing music. I play *Garden of Serenity* by David and Steve Gordon.

Suggested Script

Sit comfortably and allow yourself to focus on your breath. Every time you breathe in, feel peace and relaxation entering your body; every time you breathe out, feel stress and tension leaving your body. Breathe in peace and relaxation, and breathe out tension and stress.

Perhaps your relaxing breath has a color to it. Notice the color of relaxation and peace. Feel the color of relaxation and peace as it touches all the parts of your body with your in-breaths. Notice how good it feels.

Notice the color of stress and tension as it leaves your body. Feel the relaxing breaths fill your body with peace and allow that relaxing color to wash out the stress and tension. Release the stress and tension on the out-breaths. Continue to breathe in peace and relaxation and breathe out stress and tension.

You might find that this process continues on its own as you continue to breathe normally throughout the rest of the day or night. You might find that just from breathing normally and naturally your body begins to feel more relaxed and you feel a sense of peace inside. You might even notice that some of your feelings of stress and tension simply melt away.

And any time you feel an urge to act upon your impulses, you can find it easy to take a deep breath and feel the same relaxed peaceful feeling you feel right now. You can find it easy to make wise choices about your behaviors. And any time you think a stress-producing thought, you can find it easy to breathe in relaxation and breathe out the stress, allowing yourself to enjoy a peaceful, stress-free day or night.

And you can practice that right now. Imagine being in a situation where in the past you might have felt like acting out impulsively. Imagine being in that situation now and taking a deep, relaxing breath. Notice how easily you can breathe out the urge and find yourself acting wisely.

Any time you think a stress-producing thought, you can find it easy to breathe in relaxation and breathe out the stress, allowing yourself to enjoy a peaceful, stress-free time.

Now notice yourself in a situation where in the past you might have felt stressed about something. Imagine breathing in relaxation and peace, and breathing out the stress, finding it easy to let go of the stressful feelings.

I am going to ask you to continue breathing in peace and relaxation and breathing out stress and tension. And as I turn down the music, you can bring your awareness back into this room and open your eyes, relaxed and stress free.

Follow-Up Questions

- Ask if anyone wants to share.

- After each share, ask the person how it can help them in their life.

⅋ WISE ONE JOURNEY

Begin by asking the group members questions, such as: "If I gave you a magic wand and you could change anything in your life so that you would never have to come back to a place like this, what behavior would you change?" They might answer, "my anger."

Music

Use relaxing music. I play *Sacred Earth Drums* by David and Steve Gordon.

Suggested Script

We are going to go on an imaginary journey to meet your inner wise one, who may be a person or may be an animal. Whatever form your wise one takes today, you will be able to ask questions and receive answers. You will be able to gain awareness of how to connect with your wise one when you want to. You will be more in touch with your own Wise Mind, your inner knowing and intuition.

Make yourself comfortable. You can close your eyes or keep them open. As you hear the sound of the music and the sound of my voice, you can begin to relax, knowing that you can make any adjustments at any time to be comfortable.

Imagine waves of relaxing energy flowing through your body. Invite these waves of relaxation to move in through the top of your head, relaxing your scalp, relaxing your eyes and your cheeks and your jaw. You might notice if the relaxing energy has a color, and notice how it feels as it reaches all the different parts of your body. And as these waves of relaxing energy move down further into your body, you can find it easy to relax your neck muscles, relaxing your shoulders and your arms all the way down to your fingertips. With every breath you take you can relax even deeper inside. Allow these relaxing waves of energy to move down your back where any stress or tension can easily melt away. And now, you can invite these waves of relaxation to move down from your waist to your hips, and from your hips down your legs all the way down to the bottom of your feet… From the top of your head to the bottom of your feet, your body has nothing to do now but relax and let go.

Imagine walking in a natural place. You can feel your feet touching the ground. You can feel the temperature of the air on your skin. You can hear the sounds of nature all around you.

You can smell the scent of the outdoor air. You can see whatever there is to see in your natural place. Allow the music to take you to a place that feels very safe and very good to you. Feel just how good it feels to be in your own special and safe place.

And in your safe and special place today, perhaps you can begin to sense the presence of a wise one here with you. Your wise one might be a person or it might be an animal. Whichever it is, your wise one feels very safe and very wise and has a message for you today that can help you in your life. Notice what the message is. Spend some time asking questions and receiving answers from your inner wise one. (Pause.)

You can connect with your inner wise one anytime you want to or need to, easily. You can remember everything you want to remember about your experience today. You can return easily to this place in your inner world whenever you want to. And as you breathe, begin to bring your awareness back to being in a room filled with people. As I turn down the music and count from one to five, you can come back into the room here feeling alert, awake, and alive.

(Count from one to five with increasing volume and speed.)

Follow-Up Questions

+ Ask people to raise their hand if they got a good message from their wise one.

+ Ask if anyone wants to share.

+ After each share ask the person how it can help them in their life.

Examples

A group member who is suicidal: "My wise one was a goddess and the message was 'live.' Whenever I feel numb and hopeless, I know exactly where to go now."

A group member who wanted to handle anger in new ways: "That was awesome! I feel like I've got an avenue for handling my anger. I have a place to go to calm down. I will use it whenever I feel like life sucks."

A group member who wanted to deal with his anger: "When I feel depressed, I can go there and be undepressed. If I'm mad, I can go there. My message was on how to keep out of trouble and accomplish what I want."

A group member who felt hopeless got the message: "Only by walking through the shadows can one come through to the light. Never stop trying; you can always turn around your life."

SUCCESS

Begin by asking the group members: "What would you like to be successful at?" or "What is your dream?"

Today you will have a chance to practice being successful at whatever your dream is. Maybe it's handling your anger in new ways. Maybe it's learning a new way to deal with your urge to engage in a problem behavior. Maybe it's being successful at being a professional of some sort: a doctor or a veterinarian or a teacher or a crime scene investigator. Maybe it has to do with getting along better with someone, getting a job, doing well at school. Think about what your dream is, and you will now have an opportunity to experience being successful at that.

Music

Use relaxing music. I play *Sacred Earth Drums* by David and Steve Gordon.

Suggested Script

Make yourself comfortable. You can close your eyes or keep them open. As you hear the sound of the music and the sound of my voice, you can begin to relax, knowing that you can make any adjustments at any time to be comfortable.

Imagine waves of relaxing energy flowing through your body. You can invite these waves of relaxation to move in through the top of your head, relaxing your scalp, relaxing your eyes and your cheeks and your jaw. And as these waves of relaxing energy move further down your body, you can find it easy to relax your neck muscles, your shoulders, and your arms all the way down to your fingertips. With every breath you take, you can relax even deeper inside. Allow these relaxing waves of energy to move down your back where any stress or tension can easily melt away. And now, you can invite these waves of relaxation to move down from your waist to your hips, and from your hips all the way down your legs to the bottom of your feet... From the top of your head to the bottom of your feet, your body has nothing to do now but relax and let go.

Imagine walking in a natural place. You can feel your feet touching the ground. You can feel the temperature of the air on your skin. You can hear the sounds of nature all around you.

You can smell the scent of the outdoor air. You can see whatever there is to see in your natural place. Allow the music to take you to a place that feels very safe and very good to you. Feel just how good it feels to be in your own special and safe place.

And in your safe and special place today, perhaps you can begin to sense the presence of a wise one here with you. Your wise one might be a person or it might be an animal. Whichever it is, your wise one feels very safe and very wise and has a message for you today that can help you in your life. Notice what the message is. Spend some time asking questions and receiving answers from your inner wise one. (Pause.)

And now allow your wise one to take you into the future to see the future successful you. The future you who has already learned a new way to handle your anger, or the you who is free of all self-harming behaviors.[1] The you who has already succeeded at whatever it is you said you wanted to succeed at when you were asked at the beginning of this group. Become that future successful you now, and feel what it feels like to have accomplished your goal. Notice how it feels in your body. Notice how you are acting, what you are doing differently. Notice the people around you, what you are wearing, and all the details you can notice. (Pause.) And any time you think of this goal, you can remember how it feels to have already accomplished it, and you can find it easy to achieve it.

Now once again find yourself with your wise one in your own safe/special place, as your present-day self. You can talk to your wise one, perhaps asking about the best way for you to get from where you are now to where you want to be to succeed.

Know that you can easily remember everything you want to remember about your journey here today. You can return easily to this place in your inner world whenever you want to. You can connect with your inner wise person whenever you need to. And as you breathe, begin to bring your awareness back to being in a room. Begin to be aware of the presence of other people. As I turn down the music and count from one to five, you can come back into the room, feeling alert, awake, and alive.

(Count from one to five with increasing volume and speed.)

---

1   In an outpatient DBT group the clients go home after group, and may not have any support, so it is not advised to talk explicitly about harming yourself in case this triggers urges to do harmful things. You should replace or omit the reference to self-harm when working with an outpatient group.

Follow-Up Questions

- Ask people to raise their hand if they got a good message from their wise one.

- Ask them to raise their hand if they had an experience of being successful.

- Ask if anyone wants to share.

- After each share ask the person how it can help them in their life.

Example

A group member who wanted to take the steps to achieve her goals but felt that something was in the way:

> I was at my special place where the rock formation in the woods is when my bear wise being came to me and told me "It's storming now, but you'll make it through the rain." He took me into the future and let me see myself in a black outfit with a microphone on stage speaking to the people as a motivational speaker. And I told myself that I know what I gotta do—stay goal oriented and one day I'll be there.

This was the inspiration for the song *I'm Gonna Make It* featured on the *You'll Make it Through the Rain!* CD and downloadable from www.jkp.com/voucher using the code HUUWAHE.

SONGS

YOU'LL MAKE IT THROUGH THE RAIN!

The following five songs are on the CD *You'll Make It Through the Rain!* and can be downloaded from www.jkp.com/voucher using the code HUUWAHE.

+ *The Roller Coaster Ride*

+ *The Message*

+ *The System Song*

+ *I'm Gonna Make It*

+ *Pros and Cons*

Included in the following pages are instructions, reproducible lyric sheets, and guitar chords for each of these songs. Permission to reproduce lyric sheets for therapeutic use is granted.

❀ THE ROLLER COASTER RIDE
Main Goal

This song teaches people how to gain self-awareness and to bring themselves into Wise Mind when on the road to impulsivity. It exemplifies mindfulness. It reinforces the idea that it's not too late to stop and think and take the wise action.

DBT Skills that Are Strengthened

When you present this activity, modify your approach based on which skill you are highlighting.

Core mindfulness: This song incorporates the What Skills of Observe, Describe, and Participate and can teach the concept of Wise Mind versus Emotion Mind.

Distress tolerance: This song uses distraction with ACCEPTS (Activities, Contributing, Thoughts). During discussion, one can identify Self-Soothing skills, TIPP, and/or STOP. Pros and Cons can be explored through disruptive urges versus distress tolerance skills.

Emotion regulation: Through highlighting the model for describing emotions, the skill of understanding and naming emotions can be practiced by listening for the emotion, body reactions, and urges. The lyrics to the last verse can be used for demonstrating how to Check the Facts and Problem Solve, and the value of Opposite Action.

Instructions

1. Explain that when we get overwhelmed by our emotions, there is a point of no return (like a roller coaster) where we act impulsively, reactively, and instinctively, without any thought of consequences, and we don't even care. How can we get out of the grip of our emotions and make a wise choice about our behavior that won't leave us regretting something we did?

2. Before playing the song, ask group members to listen for the DBT skills that are in the song. After listening, go through the lyric sheet and/or listen again and stop the music in the following places.

   - After the first verse, ask, "What mind am I in?" (Emotion Mind).

   - After the first chorus, ask, "What does this mean? (I know I'm overwhelmed by my emotions right now; that I feel urges to act out and I don't care, but it's not too late to choose wisely.)

   - After the second verse, ask, "What is this verse telling us?" (I'm noticing what's happening with me—the skill of Observing and Describing. This gets me out of the grip of emotions. Then I'm able to choose a wise behavior to take care of myself, and I participate effectively.)

   - After the third verse, ask, "What else could I do that would be wise?" (If you're playing this on the guitar, you can sing their answers into the song instead of the lyrics on the page for the third verse or in a fourth verse.)

   - Ask, "What skills have we used here?" (Distraction, Accumulate Positive Emotions, or Self-Soothe.)

Responses

- "I wish I had heard this song before I had my family visit. I would have handled things differently."

- "Yeah, I wish I had heard it before too. If I'd heard *The Roller Coaster Ride* song before I acted out that night it would have gotten me to think twice before I did. Hopefully, before I go off ever, I can recite this song in my head."

The Roller Coaster Ride

Somebody treated me unfair
I know I really shouldn't care
But I feel like doing something
    mean
I don't care if it's right or wrong

Oh, here comes the roller coaster ride
I feel the anger swell inside
It's not too late
To be wise

So emotions don't control me
I notice what's happening with me
Hot tears rolling down my face
My heart's beginning to race
My thoughts are those of revenge
Maybe I should relax with my
    friends instead

Oh, here comes the roller coaster ride
I feel the anger swell inside
It's not too late
To be wise

Maybe I should go ride my bike
Or I could go for a hike
Walk outside and listen to the brook
I could read a good book...
Run real fast until the anger's gone
Or play guitar and sing you a song

Oh, here comes the roller coaster ride
I feel the anger swell inside
It's not too late
To be wise
It's not too late
To be wise

The Roller Coaster Ride

```
G         C          G
Somebody treated me unfair
G         C          G
I know I really shouldn't care
D
But I feel like doing something
   G
   mean
D                    C  G
I don't care if it's right or wrong
```

```
G                   C        G
Oh, here comes the roller coaster ride
G         C        G
I feel the anger swell inside
D        G
It's not too late
D    G
To be wise
```

```
G                   C        G
Oh, here comes the roller coaster ride
G         C        G
I feel the anger swell inside
D        G
It's not too late
D    G
To be wise
```

```
G         C          G
So emotions don't control me
G              C          G
I notice what's happening with me
D                        G
Hot tears rolling down my face
D                    G
My heart's beginning to race
D                    G
My thoughts are those of revenge
D
Maybe I should relax with my
      C        G
      friends instead
```

```
G                   C        G
Maybe I should go ride my bike
G      C      G
Or I could go for a hike
D                              G
Walk outside and listen to the brook
D                    G
I could read a good book...
D                      G
(add your own lines here)
```

```
D                            G
Run real fast until the anger's gone
D                    C  G
Or play guitar and sing you a song
```

```
G                   C        G
Oh, here comes the roller coaster ride
G         C        G
I feel the anger swell inside
D        G
It's not too late
D    G
To be wise
D        G
It's not too late
D    G
To be wise
```

�֍ THE MESSAGE

Main Goal

This song starts out by validating the experience of those who feel they are in very hopeless situations and/or who self-harm in any way (this can include overeating, drinking, impulsive shopping, etc., as well as actually cutting or suicidal behavior). It then offers skills for change or resolution. It was written with the idea of meeting the listeners where they are and then leading them to where they could be. Positive words of encouragement and affirmations are repeated throughout the song in order to plant them in the listener's mind and to teach self-encouragement and cheerleading.

DBT Skills that Are Strengthened

When you present this activity, modify your approach based on which skill you are highlighting.

Core mindfulness: Through listening to the song, one can practice the What Skills of Observe, Describe, and Participate. The discussion can reinforce the concept of Wise Mind versus Emotion Mind, and the How Skills of being Non-Judgmental, Effective, and One-Mindful.

Distress tolerance: This song uses distraction with ACCEPTS (Activities, Contributing, Thoughts). During discussion, one can identify Self-Soothing skills, TIPP, and/or STOP. Pros and Cons can be explored through disruptive urges versus distress tolerance skills. The chorus reinforces IMPROVE with Encouragement.

Emotion regulation: The lyrics could be used to explore how to manage upsetting emotions. Discussion of the song can lead to strengthening the skills of Check the Facts, Problem Solving, and Opposite Action.

Interpersonal effectiveness: Discussing the lyrics can lead to reinforcing the Validation aspect of GIVE, as well as growing ways to act with self-respect, reflecting FAST.

Instructions

1. Instruct group members to listen mindfully to the song as they will be asked which part is their favorite.

2. After listening to this song, ask the group members which of the lines felt the best for them to hear.

3. Discuss the skill of positive encouragement that we give ourselves.

4. Group members can save the lyrics sheets and underline the lyrics that are meaningful to them.

Responses

+ "This song really moves me. It helps me out a lot. I wish I could listen to it every day because I really think it would change my life and the way I think about myself."

+ "Can I keep the lyrics? Will you bring me a copy of the CD?"

+ "I like the line 'She wanted to self-harm, not knowing of her charm' because other people see my charm but not the problems I feel inside."[1]

+ "I like the line 'She tried to get rid of the pain she felt inside' because it explains me and it makes me feel good to know somebody else feels the same."

+ "I like 'When your mind is set, there's nothing you can't do' because it makes me feel like I can do anything if I put my mind to it."

+ "I like 'You deserve the best, you can make it through the rest, you're special and you really ought to know.' I want to feel special and I do deserve the best."

---

1   In an outpatient DBT group the clients go home after group, and may not have any support, so it is not advised to talk explicitly about harming yourself in case this triggers urges to do harmful things. You should replace or omit the reference to self-harm when working with an outpatient group. For example, substitute the following lyrics into the song: "Her life was such a mess, it put her to the test, she was afraid of what was next. She walked into harm, not knowing of her charm, she ignored the pain she felt inside."

The Message

Her life was such a mess
It put her to the test
She didn't really want to live the rest

They weren't always there
She wasn't treated fair
They didn't tell her sweet things
   good to hear

She wanted to self-harm[2]
Not knowing of her charm
She tried to get rid of the pain she
   felt inside

It was one deep dark night
When she first saw the light
These words began to swim within
   her head
And they said:

You deserve the best
You can make it through the rest
You're special and you really ought
   to know

Keep on being you
The way you know to do
Uniquely you is just the way to be

Go the extra mile
Live your life in style
When your mind is set, there's
   nothing you can't do

Do what you know is right

Keep your goals in sight
Be everything you know that you
   can be

But her life was oh so blue
She didn't know what else to do
So she told herself these words to
   help her through:

You deserve the best
You can make it through the rest
You're special and you really ought
   to know

Keep on being you
The way you know to do
Uniquely you is just the way to be

Go the extra mile
Live your life in style
When your mind is set, there's
   nothing you can't do

Do what you know is right
Keep your goals in sight
Be everything you know that you
   can be

So whenever she was blue
And she didn't know what to do
She'd tell herself things to help her
   through:

You deserve the best
You can make it through the rest…

---

2   In an outpatient DBT group the clients go home after group, and may not have any support,
   so it is not advised to talk explicitly about harming yourself in case this triggers urges to do
   harmful things. You should replace or omit the reference to self-harm when working with
   an outpatient group.

The Message

A   E
Her life was such a mess
A   E
It put her to the test
A   E   A E
She didn't really want to live the rest

D   A
They weren't always there
D   A
She wasn't treated fair
D   A
They didn't tell her sweet things
        E
   good to hear

A   E
She wanted to self-harm
A   E
Not knowing of her charm
A   E
She tried to get rid of the pain she
       A E
   felt inside

D   A
It was one deep dark night
D   A
When she first saw the light
D   A
These words began to swim within
       E
   her head
E
And they said:

A   D
You deserve the best
E   A
You can make it through the rest
D   E
You're special and you really ought
       A
   to know

A   D
Keep on being you
E   A
The way you know to do
D   E   A
Uniquely you is just the way to be

A   D
Go the extra mile
E   A
Live your life in style
D   E
When your mind is set, there's
       A
   nothing you can't do

A   D
Do what you know is right
E   A
Keep your goals in sight
D   E
Be everything you know that you can
       A
   be...

```
A                 E
But her life was oh so blue
A                 E
She didn't know what else to do
A                         E       A
So she told herself these words to help her through:
```

(Chorus)

```
A                 E
So whenever she was blue
A                 E
And she didn't know what to do
A                 E       A
She'd tell herself things to help her through:
```

(Chorus)

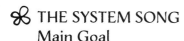 THE SYSTEM SONG
Main Goal

This song validates the experiences of those who feel trapped, whether it be in the system, in their symptoms, or in their emotions. It offers hope and an opportunity to discuss skills.

DBT Skills that Are Strengthened

When you present this activity, modify your approach based on which skill you are highlighting.

Core mindfulness: Through listening to the song, one can practice the What Skills of Observe, Describe, and Participate. The discussion can reinforce the concept of Wise Mind versus Emotion Mind, and the How Skills focusing on Effectiveness.

Distress tolerance: This song uses distraction with ACCEPTS (Activities, Contributing, Pushing Away, Thoughts). During discussion, one can identify Self-Soothing skills, TIPP, and/or STOP. The chorus reinforces IMPROVE with Imagery, Vacation, and Encouragement. Willingness and Radical Acceptance can be explored through the lyrics.

Emotion regulation: Explore how to manage upsetting emotions; review Check the Facts, Problem Solving, and Opposite Action. The chorus can be used to reinforce concepts of Building Mastery and Accumulating Positive Emotions in the long term.

Interpersonal effectiveness: The lyrics provide an opportunity for Validation. Group discussion can reinforce ways one can feel validated from GIVE, as well as growing ways to act with self-respect reflecting FAST. DEAR MAN can be applied by asking for what one may need to make a change.

Instructions

1. Listen to the song.

2. Ask for listeners' reactions to the song.

3. Discuss skills for coping with the situation.

4. Ask each group member, "What is your dream?"

5. Encourage them to hang in there. "Hold on to your dream and believe. You too can accomplish your dream."

The System Song

He said I miss my mom
And I miss my dad
And I miss my brothers too
It makes me sad, so I act bad
Doing things I shouldn't do
Deep inside, where he cried
He longed to belong to someone too
He longed to belong to someone too

Trapped in the system with
all kinds of folks
This boy has seen a lot
More than most
Trapped in the system with
all kinds of folks
This boy has seen a lot
more than most

He said I miss my mom
And I miss my dad
And I miss my brothers too
It makes me sad, don't wanna act bad
Doing things I shouldn't do
Deep inside, where he cried
He longed to belong to someone too
He longed to belong to someone too

Working the system
he does his best
to gain an hour of freedom
to call his own
Working the system
he tries his best
to gain a minute of freedom
to call his own

He said I miss my mom
And I miss my dad
And I miss my brothers too
It makes me sad, but I don't act bad
Doing things I shouldn't do
Deep inside, where he cried
He longed to belong to someone too
He longed to belong to someone too

He has strength
and he never let go
Held on to his dream and believed
He has strength
and he never let go
Achieved the dream he conceived
Achieved the dream he conceived

The System Song

G
He said I miss my mom
D
And I miss my dad
C   G
And I miss my brothers too
G   D
It makes me sad, so I act bad
           C   G
Doing things I shouldn't do
C   G
Deep inside, where he cried
C   D   C
He longed to belong to someone too
D   CG
He longed to belong to someone too

G   C
Trapped in the system with
F   D
all kinds of folks
G   C
This boy has seen a lot
D   G
more than most
G   C
Trapped in the system with
F   D
all kinds of folks
G   C
This boy has seen a lot
D   .   G
more than most

G
He said I miss my mom
D
And I miss my dad

C   G
And I miss my brothers too
G   D
It makes me sad, so I act bad
           C   G
Doing things I shouldn't do
C   G
Deep inside, where he cried
C   D   C
He longed to belong to someone too
D   CG
He longed to belong to someone too

G   C
Working the system
F   D
he does his best
G   C
to gain an hour of freedom
D   G
to call his own
G   C
Working the system
F   D
he tries his best
G   C
to gain a minute of freedom
D   G
to call his own

G
He said I miss my mom
D
And I miss my dad
C   G
And I miss my brothers too
G   D
It makes me sad, so I act bad

```
        C               G              F              D
Doing things I shouldn't do            and he never let go
C              G                       G              C              D
Deep inside, where he cried            Held on to his dream and believed
C                        D    C        G              C
He longed to belong to someone too     He has strength
D                             CG       F              D
He longed to belong to someone too     and he never let go
                                       G              C              DG
G              C                       Achieved the dream he conceived
He has strength                        G              C              DG
                                       Achieved the dream he conceived
```

❀ I'M GONNA MAKE IT!
Main Goal

This is an uplifting metaphorical song about following your heart. The song illustrates positive thinking, Opposite Action, and self-encouragement.

DBT Skills that Are Strengthened

When you present this activity, modify your approach based on which skill you are highlighting.

Core mindfulness: Through listening to the song, one can practice the What Skills of Observe, Describe, and Participate. The discussion can reinforce the concept of Wise Mind versus Emotion Mind, and the How Skills of being Non-Judgmental, Effective, and One-Mindful.

Distress tolerance: Listening to the song uses distraction with ACCEPTS (Activities, Contributing, Thoughts). The lyrics reinforce IMPROVE with Imagery and Encouragement.

Emotion regulation: The lyrics can be used to reinforce concepts of Build Mastery and Accumulating Positive Emotions in the long term.

Instructions

1. Ask group members to listen to the song with their focus on what therapeutic skills they find in it.

2. After listening, discuss what the listeners found to be therapeutic about the song and any coping skills they recognized (e.g., cheerleading, Opposite Action, Encouragement, Imagery).

3. Say to the group: "I want to take the steps to reach my goals, but I'm afraid. Do what your heart, or Wise Mind, tells you to do. Do what you know is best for you. What would you be doing if you followed your heart? What are the steps you want to take to reach your goals?"

I'm Gonna Make It!

I want to take the steps to reach my
    goals
But I'm afraid
All my life I've done what I've done
It's hard to change my ways

She was at her special place
By the rocks in the woods
When the bear
Came into view
She could have sworn that he told
    her what to do…

He said: It's storming now but you'll
    make it through the rain
You're strong and you deserve to be
    free of the pain
Just follow your heart and know
    that I'm here with you
I'll stay by your side and help you
    make it through

And she cried:

I can do it!
I know that I can
I can go any length
With you by my side
I can feel it now
So sure and so true

I'm gonna make it and to my heart
    be true

I can do it!
I know that I can
I can go any length
With you by my side
I can feel it now
So sure and so true
I'm gonna make it and to my heart
    be true

She was watchin' all the birds
And felt the spray of the waterfall
She spied a butterfly purple and
    blue
It said: Do what your heart tells you
    to do
Do what you know is the best for
    you

It said: I was a caterpillar
Crawling on the ground
I followed my heart
And cocooned all around
Now I can fly free and reach to any
    height
Remember everything will be all
    right

And she cried:

I can do it!
I know that I can
I can soar to any height
Just like you butterfly
I can feel it now
So sure and so true
I'm gonna make it
and to my heart be true

I can do it!
I know that I can
I can soar to any height
Just like you butterfly
I can feel it now
So sure and so true
I'm gonna make it
and to my heart be true

Yes I'm gonna make it
and to my heart be true

I'm Gonna Make It!

C   F
I want to take the steps to reach my
  C
 goals
C G C
But I'm afraid
C   F   C
All my life I've done what I've done
C   G   C
It's hard to change my ways

C
She was at her special place
F   C
By the rocks in the woods
When the bear
      G
Came into view
C F   C
    C   G
She could have sworn that he told
      C
 her what to do…

C
He said: It's storming now but you'll
   F   C
 make it through the rain
C
You're strong and you deserve to be
 G
 free of the pain
C
Just follow your heart and know
      F   C
 that I'm here with you
C   G
I'll stay by your side and help you
     C
 make it through

 And she cried:

(Chorus A)
C
I can do it!
F   C
I know that I can

C
I can go any length
G
With you by my side
    C
I can feel it now
      F   C
So sure and so true
C
I'm gonna make it
      G   C
and to my heart be true

(Repeat chorus A)

C
She was watchin' all the birds
F   C
And felt the spray of the waterfall
C   G
She spied a butterfly purple and blue
    C   F
It said: Do what your heart tells you
    C
    to do
C   G   C
Do what you know is the best for you

C
It said: I was a caterpillar
F   C
Crawling on the ground
C
I followed my heart
G
And cocooned all around

C   F
Now I can fly free and reach to any
      C
   height
C   G   C
Remember everything will be all
   right

And she cried:

(Chorus B)
C
I can do it!
F   C
I know that I can
C
I can soar to any height
G
Just like you butterfly
C
I can feel it now
      F   C
So sure and so true
C   G
I'm gonna make it and to my heart
         C
  be true

(Repeat chorus B)

      C
Yes I'm gonna make it
G   C
and to my heart be true

❀ PROS AND CONS

Main Goal

It takes mindfulness to focus on your own part and hearing the whole. Many people say that this song gets stuck in their heads and reminds them to stop and think.

DBT Skills that Are Strengthened

Core mindfulness: Through learning and engaging in the chant, one can practice the What Skills of Observe, Describe, and Participate. The discussion can reinforce the concept of Wise Mind versus Emotion Mind. The How Skills of being Non-Judgmental, Effective, and One-Mindful are practiced as well. It takes mindful awareness to focus on your section of the chant if you are doing it as a round.

Distress tolerance: Pros and Cons is the focus of this chant. This song uses distraction with ACCEPTS (Activities, Thoughts, Senses). The STOP skill is practiced in the lyric and rhythm. Willingness is encouraged through engaging freely in the chant and body movement.

Emotion regulation: The reluctant participant can practice Opposite Action to engage in the chant. Repeated practice can strengthen Building Mastery and Accumulating Positive Emotions.

There are three parts for this song:

A: Pros and Cons
Pros and Cons

B: Think about the consequences when I feel my urges
Think about the consequences when I feel my urges

C: Stop and think
Stop and think

Instructions

1. Listen to the Pros and Cons song.

2. Read all the lines out loud together as a group.

3. Divide the group into three and assign one part to each group.

4. Tell group members to focus their attention on their part, their group, and how the parts fit together.

5. Group A says their line over and over.

6. After four repetitions of group A's lines, group B starts their part.

7. After four repetitions of group B's part, group C starts their part.

8. After several rounds, signal for group A to stop.

9. Signal group B to stop.

10. Signal group C to stop.

11. Introduce body rhythms for each group such as:

   a. Foot stomp on beats one and three for group A: Say "Pros" (along with foot stomp) and "Cons" (along with foot stomp).

   b. Slap thighs on each beat one, two, three, and four for group B: Say "Think" (with slap) "bout" (with slap) "con" (with slap) "quen" (with slap) "when" (with slap) "feel" (with slap) "urge" (with slap) "es" (with slap).

   c. Clap on beats two and four for group C: Say "Stop (then clap) and think (then clap)."

12. Make up a combination of the above using words and/or body rhythms. Say the words or just use the body rhythms. You can have one group say the words while the other groups do their body rhythms and then switch.

Pros and Cons

Pros and Cons
Pros and Cons

Think about the consequences when I feel my urges
Think about the consequences when I feel my urges

Stop and think
Stop and think

Part 2

WORKBOOK

For the Individual to Learn and Practice
DBT Skills in a Creative Way with
or without Clinician Guidance

HOW TO USE THIS WORKBOOK

The following music activities are designed to be an enjoyable and memorable way to learn, practice, and reinforce DBT skills and are available to download from www.jkp.com/voucher using the code HUUWAHE. They are written in a self-help format. Here are some ways that they can be used:

CLINICIANS

- New ideas to reinforce, practice, and enrich the learning of DBT skills.

- Engaging assignments that your clients can use on their own in between sessions to practice and strengthen skills, making DBT homework relevant, creative, and interesting.

- More ways of helping individuals who desperately need the DBT skills but may not respond well to the manualized, language-based, didactic, skills-training curriculum, e.g., "nontraditional" learners, adolescents, and so on, as well as those clients who have an aversion to learning DBT skills, thus engaging the hard-to-reach client.

- A resource for clients who want to continue their learning and practicing of the skills through music activities upon discharge.

MUSIC THERAPISTS

- Quick grab-and-go DBT-informed interventions that can be modified by you for your work with clients in your practice.

- A resource for clients so they can continue their learning and practicing of the skills through music activities upon discharge.

THERAPISTS WORKING WITH YOUTH AND SPECIAL EDUCATION TEACHERS

- Activities to do with students who have emotional regulation IEPs (Individualized Education Programs) for promoting overall engagement, and teaching the skills in a fun way the youth can resonate with.

INDIVIDUALS OF ANY AGE

- If you are participating in a DBT program, this will help you strengthen what you are learning.

- These music activities and skills lessons are written in a user-friendly, self-help format, they can help you:

  - get through difficult times when you feel overwhelmed about how you're feeling and may not know what to do to improve your situation or feel better

  - regulate extreme up-and-down emotions

  - control impulsive and harmful behaviors

  - communicate effectively with others to preserve relationships, get people to take you seriously, get what you want from others, and end destructive relationships.

- Are you a parent feeling overwhelmed or stressed? You can enjoy these activities and lessons as well. Do them with your child and/or do them for yourself.

PERSONAL GROWTH SEEKERS

- The skills are beneficial to anyone's life, and the activities are a good way to put the skills into practice.

INSTRUCTIONS

Read and follow the instructions to one lesson a week. Select a starting day and start the next lesson that same day next week. Put it on your calendar.

Absorb the skills one at a time and practice the suggested action steps. Look for places you can use the skills in your life.

As you learn, practice, and remember the DBT skills, you'll begin to find times that you can use and may need them in your life. Grow with the skills and let them support you to create a life worth living.

One more thing… If you are not working with a therapist who is teaching you DBT skills, and you feel you'd like supportive resources, visit this DBT website: https://behavioraltech.org/resources/resources-for-clients-families/#what-is-dbt.

LESSONS

Handouts: We recommend making a copy of the DBT Skills Summary that is at the beginning of this book. Use this as a guide to focus and as a reminder of what you are gaining. Let the journey begin!

UNIT 1: MINDFULNESS

LESSONS

- Mindfulness: Being Mindful

- Mindfulness: 3 States of Mind

- Mindfulness: What Skills

- Mindfulness: How Skills

MINDFULNESS: BEING MINDFUL
Introduction to Mindfulness

Define one activity you do that helps you to remain focused and present in the moment.

_____

For example: When I am learning a new song on the guitar, swimming, and so on.

Instructions

Listen to the following song: *Living In the Moment* by Jason Mraz.

As you are listening, pay attention to the lyrics and the message of the song. If you notice that your mind wanders away from this task, just gently refocus your mind on the song!

After listening to the song, ask yourself the following questions.

- What did you notice your mind doing while you were listening?

- Were you able to stay focused on the task of listening to this song the whole time? If not, did you notice getting distracted and trying to bring your attention back to the task at hand?

- Did you notice any sensations in your body? Any emotions?

- What do you think the lyrics are about?

What the Heck Is Mindfulness?

Do you ever find yourself thinking about what has already happened or what you're afraid will happen? How much time does all this thinking about the past or the future eat up in your life? It's very common to live our lives in the past and the future so much that we end up missing out on what's happening in the here and now! Imagine that you are able to live in the moment more. How would life be better for you?

List that mindful activity again that you do to help you to remain focused and present in the moment.

_____

Mindfulness helps us reconnect to our lives, emotions, thoughts, body, and the people in our lives, so we can build a life worth living.

Mindfulness is not only about staying focused but it is also about identifying when you lose that focus. Make note of the moments when you notice that you have lost focus, and bring your attention back to what you are participating in. That is mindfulness.

Notice when you are thinking of the past or the future and bring your awareness to the present. It takes practice. And more practice.

Mindfulness is at the core of everything else we will be exploring together. If you are having thoughts such as, "Ugh, I suck at staying focused, I won't be able to do this," don't fret! There are specific strategies to help you practice being more mindful that you will be learning (through music activities, of course). It does get easier with practice, we promise!

ACTION STEP FOR THIS WEEK

This week, practice being mindful and "living in the moment." Listen to this song and pay attention to the lyrics each day this week to keep you on track!

Congratulations! You have completed this activity/lesson! Celebrate by sharing your biggest takeaway with a friend or your therapist, or through journaling. It's going to lock in what you learned today.

MINDFULNESS: 3 STATES OF MIND

According to the DBT model, there are three states of mind.

1. **Reasonable Mind** deals with thinking, facts, and logic.

2. **Emotion Mind** is ruled by feelings and (often impulsive) urges.

3. **Wise Mind** is the synthesis (another word for combination or inclusion) of both reason and emotion. It's a balanced, centered, and calm place of knowing—it's intuitive. It's the state of mind we want to be in when making important decisions and to avoid acting on impulsive urges.

Instructions

1. Listen to the song *Pink Martini* by Bolero or a song that you like, using Reasonable Mind. Be analytical (not judgmental)—use just the facts. Listen to the music logically—notice all of the components of music that you hear. Notice such things as what instruments are playing, the volume, how fast or slow it is, and any changes in the music you can observe.

2. Listen to it again, and this time listen from the perspective of Emotion Mind. How does the song make you feel? Do you notice that you feel happy, sad, or some other emotion as you listen to it? Does it remind you of a person, place, thing, or another memory? What do you notice in your body? Maybe the music makes you feel relaxed in your body or tense. Do you notice any urges? Does it make you want to move?

3. The ability to integrate the two perspectives—your experience in noticing Emotion Mind and Reasonable Mind—would be your Wise Mind. Both, even if opposite, perspectives can be true at the same time.

The following activity is about learning how to access your Wise Mind. What is it? How do you find it? One way is through the use of guided imagery. If for any reason you don't feel comfortable with imaginary journeys, you can skip this one.

Go to p.62 and read the imagery script for the Wise One Journey. Record it. Close your eyes and listen to it. Another option is to ask someone to read it to you while you listen and imagine.

- What did you learn?

- Do you feel more connected to your "Wise Mind" right now in this moment?

ACTION STEP FOR THIS WEEK

This week, practice being mindful of which state of mind you are in. In moments when you notice being in Reasonable or Emotion Mind, practice accessing Wise Mind through imagery.

Congratulations! You have completed this activity/lesson! Celebrate by sharing your biggest takeaway with a friend or your therapist, or through journaling. It's going to lock in what you learned today.

MINDFULNESS: WHAT SKILLS

What Skills are meant to help you find your Wise Mind. What Skills are to:

- Observe

- Describe

- Participate

Instructions

Listen to several songs in a row on a radio station so you hear a variety of songs. Listen and draw using images and words during the songs. While listening to the music, write down what you observe about the music. What instrument sounds do you hear? Were there violins or guitars? Drums? Was it loud? Fast or slow? Notice what emotion the song evokes in you and how that emotion feels in your body. Do you have any urges or impulses to act as a result of this song? What thoughts does it bring up?

Write this down for three or four songs.

A Skill You Can Take Away from This

In this activity, you were mindfully focused on what you *observed* (taking in information at the sensory level, without description or labels), including what you heard in the music, your thoughts, emotions, body sensations, and urges, and then you *described* what you observed by putting it into words and describing it on the paper. If you followed the instructions to completion then you *participated*.

The What Skills are meant to help you find your Wise Mind. The way these skills work in a moment of distress is that through the act of mindfully *observing* what you notice in your surroundings, in your body, and in your mind...

...and in *describing* these observations (your senses, thoughts, emotions, body sensations, and urges)...

...you can step back from the urge to act immediately and instead make a wise choice in your behavior that is effective. You then *participate* in the present moment effectively and skillfully, doing what works.

Questions to Ponder

- ◆ Have you ever had an experience of acting impulsively, without thinking about it and regretting it later? That is the time to use this skill. Before you act, notice the urge to act and get into your Wise Mind. Ask yourself, "Is this a Wise Minded choice?" Observe, Describe, and Participate. Then choose the wise action and participate mindfully.

- ◆ How can you use this skill in your life?

- ◆ What situations might come up during your week where using the What Skills to find your Wise Mind may be helpful?

The Roller Coaster Song: Example of How I Used This Skill in My Life

I wrote this song when I was mad. I was triggered by someone treating me in a way that felt unfair to me. I noticed that I had thoughts of revenge, such as, "I'm really going to get back at them!" Have you ever felt that way? I'll show you how I was able to be wise instead of acting out on those thoughts.

When we are in our Emotion Mind, it can feel pretty out of control. There seems to be a point where we are ready to say, "I don't care, I'm going to act on my impulse anyway," which I liken to a roller coaster ride.

But, "It's not too late, to be wise!"

Instructions

Listen to the song *The Roller Coaster Ride* (downloadable from www.jkp. com/voucher using the code HUUWAHE) or read the lyrics below.

Somebody treated me unfair
I know I really shouldn't care
But I feel like doing something mean
I don't care if it's right or wrong

Oh, here comes the roller coaster ride
I feel the anger swell inside
It's not too late
To be wise

So emotions don't control me
I notice what's happening with me
Hot tears rolling down my face
My heart's beginning to race
My thoughts are those of revenge
Maybe I should relax with my friends instead

(Chorus)

Maybe I should go ride my bike

Or I could go for a hike
Walk outside and listen to the brook
I could read a good book...

Run real fast until the anger's gone
Or play guitar and sing you a song

(Chorus)

1. In the first verse, what state of mind am I in?

   - Reasonable

   - Emotion

   - Wise

2. In the second verse, tell me what skill I use to stop myself from acting on that impulse. (Hint: you learned about it in the previous activity.)

3. In the third verse, I think about wise things I could do instead of getting revenge, so I can release my anger and can participate effectively, doing what works. What would you add to that list for yourself? What does your Wise Mind suggest for you when you are feeling like you want to get revenge like I wanted to do at first?

Reviewing Today's Skill and How It Applies to The Roller Coaster Song

- What to do to get to Wise Mind is called What Skills.

  - Observe

  - Describe

  - Participate

As the singer of the song, I was triggered into my Emotion Mind and ready to act impulsively, but when I observed that I had hot tears rolling down my face, my heart began to race, and my thoughts were those of revenge, that led me to step back from that urge to act out and to think about what else I might do that would be wise, such as talking with a friend instead... I then thought about several other ways to participate mindfully and effectively.

ACTION STEP FOR THIS WEEK

This week, practice Observing, Describing, and Participating mindfully to get to Wise Mind. Try to start every day by practicing in low-intensity moments. Over time, it will become much easier to Observe, Describe, and Participate in moments when your emotion intensity is much higher, and you can bring yourself to Wise Mind!

Congratulations! You have completed this activity/lesson! Celebrate by sharing your biggest takeaway with a friend or your therapist, or through journaling. It's going to lock in what you learned today.

MINDFULNESS: HOW SKILLS

Have you ever noticed yourself being judgmental? We all do it. We judge ourselves and we judge others. Take a minute to think about this. A person could say, "I'm so stupid!" Which is a judgment. The fact might be, "I didn't study for my test and I got a D on it. I feel really stupid." Or in looking at someone you might think, "That person is fat," which is judgmental. The fact that you might be observing is that the person is wearing old clothes that are too big for them and seem to make them look huge.

Instructions

Listen to two versions of *Lean on Me*: the original by Bill Withers and the version from Glee. Write down what you notice. Before you start, keep in mind to describe just the facts and avoid judgmental terms. Instead of saying one of them "was awful," you could say, "The trumpets were loud and gave me a headache" (if there are trumpets for example). Be specific, factual, and non-judgmental.

Notice any differences in your observations from one version of the song to the next.

A Skill You Can Take Away from This

- We practiced the What Skills of Observe, Describe, and Participate, which helps bring us to Wise Mind.

- *How* you practice What Skills is called How Skills.

    - "Don't judge" (Non-Judgmental)

    - "Stay focused" (One-Mindful)

    - "Do what works" (Effective)

When you noticed the differences in the songs but didn't evaluate what you noticed as being good or bad, using just the facts, you were practicing being *Non-Judgmental*. How did it go?

If you were focused on one thing at a time—comparing the two versions and not multitasking while you were listening, that is the How Skill called *One-Mindful*.

You completed this activity *Effectively*, which means doing what works in the moment to help you achieve your goal. For example, if someone calls your name in the middle of your listening of the song, doing what works might be pausing the song to answer that person and then returning to your song afterwards, instead of ignoring that person, which could actually make the situation worse!

How could the How Skills be useful to you in your life?

ACTION STEP FOR THIS WEEK

This week, notice if you are being Non-Judgmental. (Don't judge yourself for being judgmental though, just notice.) Can you switch it to facts? Do you find yourself doing many things at once? Do you sometimes end up making situations worse because of acting on an emotion or digging your heels in when things feel unfair or are you choosing the wise and Effective option?

Congratulations! You have completed this activity/lesson! Celebrate by sharing your biggest takeaway with a friend or your therapist, or through journaling. It's going to lock in what you learned today.

UNIT 2: DISTRESS TOLERANCE

LESSONS

- ◆ Crisis Survival Skill: Distraction with ACCEPTS
- ◆ Crisis Survival Skill: IMPROVE the Moment
- ◆ Crisis Survival Skill: Self-Soothing
- ◆ Crisis Survival Skill: Pros and Cons
- ◆ Acceptance Skill: Radical Acceptance
- ◆ Acceptance Skill: Willingness versus Willfulness

CRISIS SURVIVAL SKILL: DISTRACTION WITH ACCEPTS

Let's start out with a little mindfulness activity:

1. Take a moment to tune in. Observe and Describe your current emotion. How do you feel in your body? What are your thoughts? Self-talk? Urges?

   _____

   _____

2. Now listen to/watch Pharrell Williams' *Happy* song/video. Notice how you feel during and after. There is no right answer. Just notice what is true for you and write it down...

   _____

   _____

3. Some people find that the *Happy* song by Pharrell Williams creates a different emotion to the one they are feeling and that it's uplifting. Did you find that? If not, what song would create a different emotional experience for you?

The following section has some ways to tolerate the distress when you're feeling like life is messed up.

WISE MIND ACCEPTS

The skill featured this week is the Wise Mind ACCEPTS skill.

I wrote this song about the Wise Mind ACCEPTS skill. Here are the lyrics. You can make up your own melody.

A is for activities, like sports or read a book. Play your music, write a poem, or maybe you can cook.

C is for contributing, be nice to someone else. Random acts of kindness help us feel good about our self.

C is for comparison; I am better now than before. Or look at someone who has it worse and you won't feel as sore.

E is different emotion like when you are feeling depressed. And you watch a movie or read a book so you're feeling something else.

P is when you push away the things that feel so bad. You come back later and deal with them when you are not so mad.

T is for the thoughts you use to fill up your head. So you're thinking about other stuff instead.

S is for sensations like ice in hand. Go for a run, or take a hot tub, or play in the sand.

ACTION STEP FOR THIS WEEK

This week find ways to practice the skill of Wise Mind ACCEPTS.

A: Activity—find an activity to do that will distract you from your stress or difficulties such as singing a song, writing a song, reading a book, playing guitar, watching a movie… What did you do?

_____

C: Contribute—do a random act of kindness. What did you do?

_____

C: Comparison—find something to compare that you are better now or at least you don't have it as bad as… For example: One day I was sick and was feeling sorry for myself. Then I talked on the phone to my friend who had Lyme disease. I thought, "Wow, at least I am in better condition than she is. That would be much worse." What did you compare your situation to?

_____

_____

Another option for this **C** is **count your blessings**. If you prefer, write some things you are grateful for in this moment.

_____

_____

E: Different emotion—what can you do to feel a different emotion? For example, watch a movie, play a song:

_____

P: Push away—were you able to take a break from obsessing about your troubles and come back to them later?

_____

T: Distract yourself with **thoughts**. For example: name as many songs as you can think of that start with the first letter of your name:

_____

S: Sensations—go for a run, take a hot tub, hold ice in your hand:

_____

Congratulations! You have completed this activity/lesson! Celebrate by sharing your biggest takeaway with a friend or your therapist, or through journaling. It's going to lock in what you learned today.

CRISIS SURVIVAL SKILL: IMPROVE THE MOMENT

This skill is for improving the moment; each letter stands for something.

I is for Imagery

Listen to the song *Some Beach* by Blake Shelton. Yes, I know it's country and you might have a judgment about country music, but listen to the lyrics anyway. Most of my clients of all ages find that it makes the point and they laugh when they hear it and request it often...

M is for Meaning

Sometimes, when things happen, at the time it seems really awful, but in time some blessing comes out of the fact that it happened. This video of Steve Jobs makes the point: https://youtu.be/UF8uR6Z6KLc (Courtesy of Stanford News Service).

P is for Prayer

Saying a mantra or writing our own blessing can help refocus. Do you have a special verse or traditional prayer?

R is for Relaxation

Taking a moment to breathe, a warm day shower, a brewed cup of tea, or an evening listening to music... engaging in relaxing moments decreases distress.

O is for One Thing in the Moment

Slow down and restart, step by step. Remember the tortoise won the race.

V is for Vacation

Through taking a time out, we refresh ourselves. A brief rest, listening to a song that "takes you away," or watching videos from far off lands can help us take a mini retreat.

E is for Encouragement

There are lots of ways we can use music for self-encouragement. The following exercises are about that.

Activity 1

1. List some songs that are encouraging to you.

   _____

   _____

   _____

2. I wrote a song called *I'm Gonna Make It* for someone I worked with. Remember the wise one journey we did in the mindfulness lesson? Well, during that journey, this person received the message, "It's storming now, but you'll make it through the rain." This song is encouraging. You can download this song from www.jkp.com/voucher using the code HUUWAHE or read the lyrics on p.80. Listen for the encouraging words and notice if the rest of the messages she got from the bear and the butterfly apply to you.

3. Here are the lyrics to another encouraging song that I wrote called *The Message* (downloadable from www.jkp.com/voucher using the code HUUWAHE). As you listen to this song, write down which lines mean the most to you.

   You deserve the best
   You can make it through the rest
   You're special and you really ought to know
   Keep on being you, the way you know to do
   Uniquely you is just the way to be
   Go the extra mile
   Live your life in style
   Be everything you know that you can be

Activity 2

1. Write your name down the edge of the page. For example:

    D

    E

    B

    O

    R

    A

    H

2. Now, write a positive word or two that starts with each letter of your name. The words can be things that you want to be true, even if you don't think they are yet. For example:

    D: Determined

    E: Enthusiastic

    B: Brilliant

    O: Organized (oh how I want this one to be true!)

    R: Real nice

    A: Authentic

    H: Happy

3. Decorate the page. Post this on your wall.

ACTION STEP FOR THIS WEEK

Practice using IMPROVE the Moment with encouragement:

1. Make a playlist of encouraging songs. Listen to encouraging songs.

2. Look at the encouraging words you wrote on the paper above (put it on your wall).

Congratulations! You have completed this activity/lesson! Celebrate by sharing your biggest takeaway with a friend or your therapist, or through journaling. It's going to lock in what you learned today.

CRISIS SURVIVAL SKILL: SELF-SOOTHING

This skill uses all of your senses.

Hearing

What's soothing to you to listen to? Rain, windchimes, water flowing, certain music? Make a list.

_____

_____

_____

_____

What elements of music do you find soothing? For example:

Male or female singers?

_____

What instruments?

_____

What style?

_____

If you enjoy relaxation music, do you like it with or without nature sounds? If with, which ones?

_____

Put together a collection of music that you find soothing.

Sight

Find relaxing images. You can find them in magazines or calendars, or do a Google search. You may consider making PowerPoint slides or watching YouTube videos with different scenery. Watch them while listening to your soothing music if you'd like.

If you have an iPad, use the "Bloom" application. Pressing on the screen creates both a tone and a color droplet, which combines both hearing and sight senses.

Taste

Get a piece of chocolate, a peppermint, or your favorite food. First, look at it. Smell it. Hear the sound of the wrapper as you unwrap it. Eat it slowly—feel how it feels on your tongue. Taste it...

Smell

Find some lotion that smells good, some bath oil, or a scented candle. Go outside and smell the roses. Smell the food cooking...

Touch

Massage the lotion into your hands and feet slowly and feel it relax you. Hug someone, or a stuffed animal. Feel a soft blanket or cloth. Pet your dog or cat.

ACTION STEP FOR THIS WEEK

Create your own personalized Self-Soothe kit. Put in it:

- your selection of "soothing music" that you can listen to when in distress

- images, photos, a PowerPoint presentation, or YouTube video you can watch while playing the music

- a piece of candy or a food bar that's wrapped up for those distress moments

- your favorite smelling lotion

- a blanket or soft cloth.

Congratulations! You have completed this activity/lesson! Celebrate by sharing your biggest takeaway with a friend or your therapist, or through journaling. It's going to lock in what you learned today.

CRISIS SURVIVAL SKILL: PROS AND CONS
Pros and Cons

A chant by Deborah Spiegel MTBC:

> Pros and Cons
> Pros and Cons
>
> Think about the consequences when I feel my urges
> Think about the consequences when I feel my urges
>
> Stop and think
> Stop and think

Instructions

1. Listen to the song (downloadable from www.jkp.com/voucher using the code HUUWAHE).

2. Listen actively, using your body.

   - During "Pros and Cons" stomp your feet.

   - During "think about the consequences" rub your hands together.

   - During "stop and think" say "stop" then clap and then point to your head.

ACTION STEP FOR THIS WEEK

Listen to the song every day this week. Teach it to at least one other person.

Congratulations! You have completed this activity/lesson! Celebrate by sharing your biggest takeaway with a friend or your therapist, or through journaling. It's going to lock in what you learned today.

ACCEPTANCE SKILL: RADICAL ACCEPTANCE

Radical Acceptance is accepting what is, rather than fighting reality.

Listen to Kelly Clarkson's song *Stronger*. Think about what you've been through that's made you stronger. It could be you've had an illness, or some sort of physical pain, or even emotional pain. Maybe someone didn't treat you the way you feel you deserve to be treated, you lost your dog, or your relationship ended. Or...

Did (or does) the pain get you down? Did you work with the pain or resist it? Did resisting the pain help or keep you struggling? Think about a situation that was emotionally and/or physically hard for you. Ask yourself those three questions and write your responses here.

_____

_____

_____

Example

Sometimes I have what they call "cluster headaches." If I focus on the pain, I suffer. It's awful. I feel sorry for myself and am in horrible pain.

But, if I focus on the fact that the pain will end in 15 minutes, focus on my breath as I breathe in deeply, and focus mindfully on the hour or few hours I have in between episodes that I feel human and alive, my life is great! It's been a constant lesson in turning the mind to the positive and in accepting the reality of what is. Yes, I can seek remedies, and do, and yet, in the moments of the pain, the only thing that works for me and gets me through it without making it worse is to practice acceptance and to focus on the positive.

What is going on in your life that you need to radically accept?

_____

_____

_____

What do you do that makes it worse?

_____

_____

_____

Radical Acceptance is an ongoing thing. In Alcoholics Anonymous, they say to take it "one day at a time," because a person can accept and commit to not drinking for a day much more easily than thinking about accepting and committing to not drinking forever. And this is their slogan, the Serenity Prayer (Niebuhr, 1951):

Grant me the serenity

to accept the things I cannot change

the courage to change the things I can

and the wisdom to know the difference.

ACTION STEP FOR THIS WEEK

Make up a melody for the serenity prayer and sing it to yourself often. Practice Radical Acceptance.

Congratulations! You have completed this activity/lesson! Celebrate by sharing your biggest takeaway with a friend or your therapist, or through journaling. It's going to lock in what you learned today.

ACCEPTANCE SKILL: WILLINGNESS VERSUS WILLFULNESS

Willingness is the ability to be accepting to life, to yourself, to change…

Have you ever found yourself stubborn? Intolerant? Not wanting to change? Controlling? Or just wanting to give up? This defines *willfulness*. It can keep us stuck.

Willingness helps us take healthy risks, embrace change, be open to ourselves and others, and recognize our limitations and abilities!

Start to pay attention to if you are being willing versus being willful.

When someone is upsetting to you, notice your body language. Do you cross your arms or allow your hands to rest down with palms up? When you notice that you are crossing your arms, for example, and you choose to switch to opening your hands with your palms up, you're using a skill called Willing Hands. This open-hands position allows us to take our world in, and believe it or not, it can help you become more willing. Try it now.

Instructions

1. Rest and sit with your hands gently at your sides or on the table in front of you, palms up.

2. Put on your favorite song and soak it in. Use mindfulness and listen. Resist urges to move—just be willing to listen and participate in how much you love this song.

3. Now put on a piece of music you have never heard, maybe Leroy Anderson's *Syncopated Clock*. Sit in the same way and soak it in. Resist urges to move—just be willing to listen and participate in hearing something different.

4. You may even challenge yourself to listen to a song you absolutely dread! Practice willingness; you may hear something new.

ACTION STEP FOR THIS WEEK

Each day this week, challenge yourself to recognize willingness versus willfulness. Practice using Willing Hands at least three times each day—when you are sitting, standing, or even lying down. Share this tip with at least one other person. Be willing to share!

Congratulations! You have completed this activity/lesson! Celebrate by sharing your biggest takeaway with a friend or your therapist, or through journaling. It's going to lock in what you learned today.

UNIT 3: EMOTION REGULATION

LESSONS

- Observing and Describing Emotions
- Decrease the Amount of Time in Unwanted Emotions: Check the Facts
- Changing Unwanted Emotions: Opposite Action
- Reducing Vulnerability to Emotion Mind: Accumulating Positives
- Reducing Vulnerability to Emotion Mind: Building Mastery
- Reducing Vulnerability to Emotion Mind: Coping Ahead
- Reducing Vulnerability to Emotion Mind: PLEASE

OBSERVING AND DESCRIBING EMOTIONS

According to the DBT model, there are four goals in learning to regulate our emotions.

1. Understand and name your emotions.
2. Decrease the amount of time one has to spend in unwanted emotions.
3. Decrease the ease (vulnerability) with which one can fall into Emotion Mind and ability to bounce back from it (resilience).
4. Decrease emotional suffering—manage extremes so that we can use distress tolerance.

Let's work on understanding and naming our emotions by making an "emotions journal."

Instructions

1. Let's pick five emotions that you feel are "uplifting" to you and five that are "upsetting." List one on the top of each page—for example, "Happy" on one and "Sad" on another.

2. Let's search… Ask yourself to list as many songs as you can for each emotion. If you can, play these songs as you work on each emotion.

3. Ask yourself: What situations can prompt that emotion? For example, for joy: seeing a sunrise, a friend's phone call.

4. Now, ask yourself what you say to yourself when you are experiencing that emotion. For example, for joy: "I can relax," "I am loved," "I succeeded."

5. One more question… What are you noticing in your body related to that emotion? For example, for joy: "I notice that my heart is beating quickly, I am open, I am giggling."

6. We're not done yet… How do you express this emotion? For example: "When I feel joy, I smile, I jump up and down, I am quiet."

7. Last question… What happens after this emotion starts? For example: "When joy starts, I am nicer to people, I worry that it will not happen again, I see the positive things."

When we begin to understand emotions, we can begin to understand what prompts them and how to share them, and understand ourselves. We are better able to control our emotional responses and regulate our emotions.

When you are confused, you can look back at your journal. When you want to change an emotion, you can look back at your journal. When you want to share an emotion, you can look back at your journal.

ACTION STEP FOR THIS WEEK

This week, practice being aware of which emotions you are experiencing and find helpful or hurtful. Add to your journal throughout the week. Understanding our emotions is the first step! Keep expanding your awareness.

Congratulations! You have completed this activity/lesson! Celebrate by sharing your biggest takeaway with a friend or your therapist, or through journaling. It's going to lock in what you learned today.

DECREASE THE AMOUNT OF TIME IN UNWANTED EMOTIONS: CHECK THE FACTS

According to the DBT model, there are four goals in learning to regulate our emotions.

1. Understand and name your emotions.

2. Decrease the amount of time one has to spend in unwanted emotions.

3. Decrease the ease (vulnerability) with which one can fall into Emotion Mind and ability to bounce back from it (resilience).

4. Decrease emotional suffering—manage extremes so that we can use distress tolerance.

Let's work on changing how long to stay in an unwanted emotion.

Instructions

1. Listen to *The Roller Coaster Ride* (downloadable from www.jkp.com/voucher using the code HUUWAHE) or read the lyrics on p.69.

2. Can you remember what made her mad? Someone treated her unfairly.

3. Can you think of a time that you were mad? If not go back to the last lesson... look in your emotions journal.

4. Now ask yourself: Is it reasonable that someone may feel mad when treated unfairly? If my teacher gave me a poor grade, yet I met all the requirements—*yes*! It is reasonable and my emotion "fits the facts."

Let's work on rewriting *The Roller Coaster Song.*

"Insert your prompting event"
I know I really shouldn't care
But I feel like doing something mean
and I don't care if it is right or wrong

Oh, here comes the roller coaster ride
I feel the anger swell inside
But it's not too late
To be wise

So emotions don't control me
I notice what's happening with me
"Insert some of your body changes"
"Insert some of your body changes"
My thoughts are those *"Insert some of your thoughts"*
Maybe I should "WAIT"

Wait! I haven't learned what to do with that feeling yet...

Often, when we have a prompting event it can lead to a *thought* and/ or an interpretation about this event, which then leads to an *emotion*. Sometimes we misinterpret the prompting event. Observing our thoughts and interpretations of these thoughts by checking the facts can help us to change our *emotion*.

Let's agree that it is *okay* and *reasonable* to feel angry when I am treated unfairly. Wise Mind reminds me that it is okay and reasonable to feel angry.

Emotions can fit the facts. For example, when I am in danger because a bear is chasing me in the woods—I am afraid and the fear is justified. Let's practice:

A time *fear* had fit the facts for me:

Example: "I was in a car accident and afraid I had hurt someone else."

Your example:

_____

_____

A time *anger* had fit the facts for me:

Example: "My son was called a horrible name by a classmate."

Your example:

_____

_____

A time *disgust* had fit the facts for me:

Example: "I saw a news story about a child being bullied and other children laughing."

Your example:

_____

_____

A time *love* had fit the facts for me:

Example: "My kitten curled up in my lap and started to purr."

Your example:

_____

_____

A time *joy* had fit the facts for me:

Example: "I read an article about my brother's successes in college."

Your example:

_____

_____

A time *sadness* had fit the facts for me:

Example: "I lost a job I really enjoyed because the site closed."

Your example:

_____

_____

It is really important to realize that it is okay to feel what we feel, and that sadness, joy, anger, and all the other emotions we experience can be justified and make sense.

But sometimes, if our emotion is based on a misinterpretation, it is unjustified. And that is when we use the skill called Check the Facts! Here's how it works:

> Sandy, a 16-year-old girl, came into the kitchen one morning, and her mother yelled at her (prompting event). Sandy interpreted this to mean, "My mother hates me!" This led to her experiencing a burning sensation in her chest (body sensations). She found that her fists were clenched (body language) and that she had the urge to run into her room and slam the door (action urge). Which she did (action). She let herself calm down for a while, thought about it, and asked herself the following questions...

Ask Yourself

1. Am I making any interpretations, judgments, or assumptions about the prompting event? If so, seek more information. Ask questions. Think of other possible interpretations.

2. Am I assuming a threat? If so, ask yourself how likely it is that the threatening event will occur. What is another possible outcome?

3. What's the worst that could happen? Imagine coping effectively with the worst-case scenario!

4. Does my emotion and its intensity fit the facts?

For Sandy, when she asked her mom questions to gain more information, she found out her mom had just lost her job! Therefore, Sandy's assumption that her mother hated her was a misinterpretation. This reduced the intensity of Sandy's anger.

Let's go back to our song. Would the song be different if one interpreted being treated unfairly differently? What if the person didn't know they were being unfair, or had a reason that had nothing to do with me? Examining our thoughts can help change our emotions.

Somebody treated me unfair
I'm sure she was totally unaware
Maybe she just had a bad day
I'll check the facts to see what she has to say
Oh, here comes the roller coaster ride

I feel the anger swell inside
But it's not too late
To be wise
And *Check the Facts*!

A Skill You Can Take Away from This

This activity has been about recognizing that our thoughts can influence our emotions and that expanding perceptions can help us reduce the intensity of unwanted emotions.

> ## ACTION STEP FOR THIS WEEK
>
> Challenge yourself to write your own song or poem about another emotion. Add your poems/songs to your journal throughout the week.
>
> Continue to practice being aware of which emotions you are experiencing and find helpful or hurtful. Challenging interpretations can work. Practice.

Congratulations! You have completed this activity/lesson! Celebrate by sharing your biggest takeaway with a friend or your therapist, or through journaling. It's going to lock in what you learned today.

CHANGING UNWANTED EMOTIONS: OPPOSITE ACTION

According to the DBT model, there are four goals in learning to regulate our emotions.

1. Understand and name your emotions.

2. Decrease the amount of time one has to spend in unwanted emotions.

3. Decrease the ease (vulnerability) with which one can fall into Emotion Mind and ability to bounce back from it (resilience).

4. Decrease emotional suffering—manage extremes so that we can use distress tolerance.

Let's work on changing unwanted emotional urges through Opposite Action.

Instructions

Listen to three different types of music: one R&B, one pop, and one classical in nature. Observe any movement inside your body (e.g., toe tapping, swaying) and any emotions that may come up (e.g., "I am experiencing sadness when I hear this song"). Fill in the blanks below.

R & B song:

_____

Physical urges:

_____

_____

_____

Emotions that I experienced:

_____

_____

_____

Pop song:

_____

Physical urges:

_____

_____

_____

Emotions that I experienced:

_____

_____

_____

Classical piece:

_____

Physical urges:

_____

_____

_____

Emotions that I experienced:

_____

_____

_____

An urge is a strong desire or impulse. Like music, we have emotional urges. When we feel fear, a common action urge is to run away or avoid. However, that may not always be helpful or possible.

For example, if I have to present a speech to a group or a class, and I am afraid, my urge might be to hide. My fear is unjustified, because speaking is not going to hurt me. If I had to face a lion and the lion could hurt me, the fear of the lion would be justified. So in my example, since speaking is not physically dangerous, the Opposite Action to my emotion of fear would be to speak anyhow. Feel the fear and do the talk. Maybe I present my talk to a friend first. Then to two people. Then to four people. Until I am taking Opposite Action and speaking to the entire group.

Let's practice an urge: think of something that really makes you angry. Now play what that sounds like on a drum or on your bed. Wow. Attack! That is our urge. Is that helpful? What is the opposite? Play that on your drum or on your bed. Gentle. By taking Opposite Action, if we approach situations that make us angry with gentle kindness, we are more likely to feel more satisfied and successful. It's more likely to have an effective outcome.

Let's do another: think of sadness. What color is it? Get out some watercolors and let sadness flow to your paper. Sadness tends to make us withdraw or isolate. What is the Opposite Action to isolating? Paint it. Did you change the color? Did you make it move? Get active and challenge yourself to decrease isolation by socializing.

A Skill You Can Take Away from This

This activity has been about acknowledging our emotional urges, noticing the action urge associated with that emotion, and challenging ourselves to explore whether the Opposite Action to that emotion would be more effective.

ACTION STEP FOR THIS WEEK

This week, continue to practice being aware of emotions you are experiencing and whether Opposite Action can be more productive. Start thinking about patterns in your emotions and whether some arise more than others—particularly if you are tired or hungry.

Congratulations! You have completed this activity/lesson! Celebrate by sharing your biggest takeaway with a friend or your therapist, or through journaling. It's going to lock in what you learned today.

REDUCING VULNERABILITY TO EMOTION MIND: ACCUMULATING POSITIVES

What do you do to create positive emotions? What is pleasurable to you? Make a list and do something on that list each and every day.

Here are some ideas for using music to build positives. You can:

- play music

- listen to music

- dance to music

- build and achieve mastery by practicing music on an instrument or learning to sing a song

- set goals of learning new songs and new instruments

- perform.

If you aren't interested in learning to play an instrument or sing, think of something else you would like to accomplish and take the first step. What is it for you?

Affirmations

One way to create positives is to write affirmations. You can even make a song out of them.

An affirmation is a positive statement, in the present tense, as if it is happening now.

The problem with negative thoughts is that they can become self-fulfilling prophecies. We talk ourselves into believing that we're not good enough. And, as a result, these thoughts drag down our personal lives, our relationships, and our careers.

But, if we deliberately use positive thoughts about ourselves, the effect can be just as powerful but far more helpful. (Hence an affirmation.) When you repeat the positive affirmations often, and believe in them, you can start to make positive changes. (Mind Tools 1996–2019)

Instructions

1. I'm going to share a song I wrote for someone I worked with. It's called *I'm Gonna Make It*. Remember the wise one journey we did in the mindfulness lesson? Well, during that journey, this person received the message, "It's storming now, but you'll make it through the rain." Listen to the *I'm Gonna Make it* song (downloadable from www.jkp.com/voucher using the code HUUWAHE). This song uses a lot of affirmations, as well as being encouraging. It's one way to build positives. Listen for the affirmations and make note of any of the messages she got from the bear and the butterfly that apply to you.

   I can do it
   I know that I can
   I can go any length, with you by my side
   I can feel it now
   So sure and so true
   I'm gonna make it
   And to my heart be true

2. Listen to the song by The Mrs called *I'm Enough* and watch the video. Write down your thoughts and emotions as you hear and watch it.

   Now it's your turn to write a song… You will be painting a picture of what you want to be true as if it already is. You will be using affirmations to build positive emotions. By telling yourself you can succeed, you can. Thoughts can either limit us or create the results we want. Become aware of your thoughts and allow positive thoughts to dominate your thinking. If you notice your mind wandering to the negative, just bring your focus back to something positive. Fill in the blanks below.

I deserve:

_____

I am willing to:

_____

I am learning to:

_____

How does it feel to say these statements? (Positive, encouraging, empowering?)

3. Write out three negative things you tell yourself. And then turn them into positive affirmations. For example:

Negative thoughts:

- I always make mistakes.

- I am stupid.

- I never do anything right.

Affirmation:

- I am getting better every time I do this.

- I am learning every day.

- It's okay to make mistakes.

- Willingness to fail leads to success.

_____

_____

_____

_____

_____

_____

_____

_____

_____

_____

4. Paint a picture in words describing how you want to feel and what you want to achieve, as if it's happening right now. You can use your positive affirmation sentences you filled in above or you can make up different affirmations. This can look like a song, a rap, a paragraph, or

some sentences using affirmations. Or you can select a song you like and know already, and substitute your lyrics into the song.

5. Look for a karaoke version of a song for background music to read or rap your story, poem, or song to. Or you can sing or read your song without music.

6. Record your song.

ACTION STEP FOR THIS WEEK

1. Make a list of things you can do that will create positive experiences for you and do at least one thing from your list each day.

2. Finish writing your affirmation song and sing it to yourself every day.

Congratulations! You have completed this activity/lesson! Celebrate by sharing your biggest takeaway with a friend or your therapist, or through journaling. It's going to lock in what you learned today.

REDUCING VULNERABILITY TO EMOTION MIND: BUILDING MASTERY

Did you ever sit down at a piano, maybe for the first time when you didn't know anything about how to play it, and after you picked at the notes, or someone showed you a few things, you figured out how to play a song? How did that make you feel? Did you say to someone, "Listen to this!"

Think of a child learning to ride a bicycle for the first time. They try and try until they get it, and yay! Check out the smile on their face.

Building Mastery is when you achieve the thing that you set your mind on accomplishing. Maybe it's something you are new at, and you accomplish it! It helps build positive emotions you can draw on when things get tough.

Instructions

Challenge yourself to doing something new. Make sure whatever you pick is not too easy to do, because that wouldn't give you that same challenge and pride in accomplishment. And don't pick something too difficult for you either, because that might backfire and make you feel down about yourself. Pick something challenging yet do-able. Take the first step and practice, practice, practice it.

Example

1. Go online, to a music store, or into your music collection and find a book or video that teaches guitar. Learn to play one chord on the guitar. Celebrate when you get it!

2. If you have that down, then learn two chords on the guitar and practice changing from one chord to the other until you get that down.

3. Learn three chords on the guitar and practice changing from one to the others.

4. Already know how to do that? Sing a song while playing those three chords on the guitar.

Feel the excitement and pride in yourself as you master *each step*. This is mastery.

ACTION STEP FOR THIS WEEK

1. Choose something you would like to master. What is it? What is your first step? Take the first step. Notice how you feel.

2. Practice until you get better and better at it and feel good about it.

Congratulations! You have completed this activity/lesson! Celebrate by sharing your biggest takeaway with a friend or your therapist, or through journaling. It's going to lock in what you learned today.

REDUCING VULNERABILITY TO EMOTION MIND: COPING AHEAD

As you have faced challenges, have you ever thought. "I saw that coming!"? Or have you noticed that every time you have a problem behavior it has the same prompting event?

Coping Ahead helps us be prepared for these moments. We can cope ahead so we are prepared to react in a new way when faced with situations that we know usually trigger us. It can help us with tough stuff in life.

Instructions

1. Listen to the song *I Can See Clearly Now* by Jimmy Cliff.

2. Write out the lines to the first verse!

3. Did you hear it...?

    Focus on the second line of *I Can See Clearly Now*.

    The song reminds us about the tough times, and we can prepare!

Let's practice:

1. Describe a situation that may have obstacles attached to it. Be specific. Practice naming the upsetting or uplifting emotions around this upcoming situation. For example:

    Upsetting: I have to give a speech in English class. I will have to stand in front of the class and speak loudly. I always feel anxious and overwhelmed when I have to get in front of a room and I tend to engage in unhealthy behaviors to cope with my stress.

    Uplifting emotions: I want to remember the feeling that I can get when I've accomplished something difficult. When I'm done I want to feel proud of myself for having done it, and feel happy and relieved. I also want to feel proud that I didn't engage in my usual unhealthy behaviors.

2. Decide what steps you can take to prepare, cope ahead, and get through this obstacle.

    For example: I can write the speech today and practice it in a mirror and in front of supports. I can do deep breathing and visualization before class. I may have the urge to run, but I can use Opposite Action and face it!

3. Now daydream the situation as realistically as you can. Rehearse it step by step with success! If it helps, use the Success suggested script on p.64 and edit the words to include all the details you want to experience. Record it. Lie down and visualize while listening to it.

ACTION STEP FOR THIS WEEK

Make a list of challenges you anticipate this week. Practice the steps above. Listen to *I Can See Clearly Now* each time you rehearse! Visualize success.

Congratulations! You have completed this activity/lesson! Celebrate by sharing your biggest takeaway with a friend or your therapist, or through journaling. It's going to lock in what you learned today.

REDUCING VULNERABILITY TO EMOTION MIND: PLEASE

Vulnerability means being at risk of something. Emotional vulnerability means being at risk of upsetting emotions and being reactive to our urges.

Have you ever been distracted and irritable when you are hungry? Or when you didn't get enough sleep? We are more emotionally susceptible to being irritable and reactive when the PLEASE steps are not followed.

1. Treat PhysicaL illness

2. Balance Eating

3. Avoid mood-Altering substances

4. Balance Sleep

5. Get Exercise

Think of PLEASE as, "Please take care of you!"

Instructions

1. **PL: Treat PhysicaL illness:** Make a list of ways you keep yourself physically healthy and put your doctor's phone number in your cell phone.

2. **E: Balance Eating:** This week, limit or even avoid foods that you know to be unhealthy for you, such as those containing preservatives or artificial sweeteners, fast food, and sweets. Make an effort to balance your eating so you are not eating too much or too little. Try to vary the foods you eat. Add one new vegetable and one new fruit this week. Notice your water intake. Drink one extra glass of water each day.

3. **A: Avoid mood-Altering substances:** Stay away from illicit drugs and alcohol. Keep in mind that even caffeine and nicotine affect our emotions.

4. **S: Balance Sleep:** Research what a sleep routine means. Practice a relaxation meditation each evening for 15 minutes prior to bed.

5. **E: Get Exercise:** Get moving! Pick ten of your favorite upbeat tunes, put in your earbuds, and do your favorite exercise. Or walk around

your block, your house, or your local mall. Do this on at least four days this week.

ACTION STEP FOR THIS WEEK

Follow the instructions above and keep a PLEASE journal listing successes and challenges for each step (PL, E, A, S, E). Notice and add an entry for each of the emotions that you are experiencing as you are taking care of you! Practice for a week—you may just want to keep PLEASE as healthy habits for a lifetime!

Congratulations! You have completed this activity/lesson! Celebrate by sharing your biggest takeaway with a friend or your therapist, or through journaling. It's going to lock in what you learned today.

UNIT 4: INTERPERSONAL EFFECTIVENESS

LESSONS

- ◆ Asking For What You Want (DEAR MAN)
- ◆ Keeping the Relationship (GIVE)
- ◆ Keeping Your Self-Respect (FAST)

ASKING FOR WHAT YOU WANT (DEAR MAN)

Here is a formula for asking for what you want.

If you use this formula when you ask for something or need to say no to someone's request, you are more likely to get what you are asking for or have your "no" respected. This skill can also help others take your opinion more seriously, keep or even improve your relationship with the person you're asking, and keep your self-respect. DEAR MAN is an acronym, so each letter stands for something else.

Start out with DEAR.

D: Describe the Situation

Start out by giving the background rather than jumping right into asking. Talk about why you want and deserve what you are asking for. Think through all the facts that you can present to support your case. What questions do you think they will want to ask you before they say yes? Think about this ahead of time and answer the questions before they ask them. Stick to the facts and stay away from judgmental or blaming statements.

Here is an example of a teen who had her cell phone taken away and wanted to ask for it back:

I haven't had my cell phone for a month now. You took it away after the night I came home too late. I've been home and in bed by 10pm every night since then. I have good grades in all my classes now. I'm being responsible and am even applying for part-time jobs.

E: Express Your Feelings and Opinions

Explain how you feel and what you believe about the situation. For example: "I feel I have earned the privilege to have my phone back."

A: Assertively Ask or Say No

Ask directly for what you want. Not timidly and not aggressively. Assertively. Don't assume the person you're talking to will know what it is you want or are saying no to without directly stating it! Be self-confident, decisive, and assured. For example: "Will you give me back my phone now?"

R: Reinforce the Person You Are Asking

Tell the person what's in it for them to give you what you're asking for or agree to your "no." For example:

> If I had a phone I could call you and keep you posted about where I am and what I'm up to. You could reach me at all times. I'm applying for part-time jobs so that I can help you pay for the phone bill.

After asking this much, stop and listen to their response. If they say yes, you're done!

If they say no, get off the subject, or start blaming you for something… use the next part: MAN.

M: Mindful

Stay focused on your goal. Keep asking and expressing your opinion over and over. If they threaten or blame you or try to pull you into another subject, ignore that and come back to your question. For example:

They say: "You were out late and were irresponsible."

You say: "That's true, I was irresponsible and now I'm trying to demonstrate being more responsible. Therefore, can I have my phone?"

A: Appear Confident

Make eye contact, stand up straight, use a confident voice. You may not feel confident on the inside and yet you have to try and portray confidence on the outside! Fake it until you make it!

N: Negotiate

If your first assert doesn't work, negotiate for other options. Sometimes, you have to give to get. For example: "If I can't have it tonight, can I have it tomorrow?" Or, "Can I use it for an hour and build up to all day...?"

If they keep saying no, turn the tables. Ask them, "If you were in my shoes, what would you do?" Listen.

After trying all of these things, if the answer is still no, then accept the no.

To remember this formula, sing along with my DEAR MAN song (video downloadable from www.jkp.com/voucher using the code HUUWAHE):

DEAR MAN Song

DEAR MAN, DEAR MAN to ask for what you want use DEAR MAN, DEAR MAN to ask for what you want

D: Describe the current situation

E: Express your feelings and opinions

A: Assert by asking or say no

R: Reinforce the person you are asking

M: Be mindful, stay focused on your goal

A: Appear like you feel confident

N: Negotiate for other options

ACTION STEP FOR THIS WEEK

1. Think of something you want to ask someone for. Using the format above, write out a DEAR MAN script on a sheet of paper.

2. Try it with someone. Practice using the skill.

Congratulations! You have completed this activity/lesson! Celebrate by sharing your biggest takeaway with a friend or your therapist, or through journaling. It's going to lock in what you learned today.

KEEPING THE RELATIONSHIP (GIVE)
To Keep the Relationship

When you realize in an interpersonal situation that the most important goal is to maintain the relationship, use the GIVE skill. GIVE can also be added to the DEAR MAN skill if, when trying to ask for something or say no to something, you realize the relationship with the person is also important to you.

Really think about this, because sometimes even though you don't like someone or think that they are not important in your life, they may be.

For example, if you're a student and have to talk to the school principal, or if you are asking someone like the police, the judge, or your boss for something, you want to make the right impression and develop a good relationship with the person. So the way you ask them is important because they have a big influence on the outcome. A question you can ask yourself is, "How do I want the person to think about me when our conversation is over?" If you'd like for them to have respect for you and be interested in talking to you again in the future, use GIVE:

G: Gentle

Be courteous rather than attacking or judgmental. Stay away from manipulative statements such as, "I'll do 'X' if you don't."

I: Interested

Act interested in the other person's point of view. Look them in the eye. Don't interrupt or talk over them. Listen to what they are saying. You don't have to agree or disagree, just hear them; it really helps you get what you are asking for!

V: Validate

This goes along with acting interested. Let the other person know that you heard them. This is one of the most valuable relationship skills there is. Tell your mother, "I hear you saying that you don't trust me to actually pay for the phone," or whatever she says to you. You can say your response after that. When the person feels like you are hearing them, they are more likely to give you what you are asking for.

E: Easy Manner

Relax and approach with gentle humor and kindness. The well-known adage, "You catch more flies with honey than vinegar," speaks to approaching with a smile rather than a scowl or demands.

Instructions

1. Listen to the song *Peaceful Easy Feeling* by the Eagles. Here are some new lyrics to the first verse of that song written by Matthew Page, MA, MT-BC, who created this activity.

   (G)entle
   No threats, no disrespect, no judgment, my approach as gentle as
       can be
   (I)nterested
   I'll sit and listen to your thoughts and pass the day
   (V)alidate
   Your words mean something to me
   (E)asy Manner
   Followed by the chorus from *Peaceful Easy Feeling*

2. Now you get to write new lyrics to the song. Follow the example above. The most important thing is to write out your answers to the questions below. Don't worry about the music or if it fits the song exactly. Think of a current situation, something you want to ask someone for where the relationship is important to you but there is some conflict with the person. Answer the following questions:

   - What is the situation?

   - What is the conflict?

   - What's your current approach?

   - What do you think the other person is feeling?

   For example:

   - Current conflict: I recently had an argument with a friend. We had plans to go to an event together but haven't talked since the argument. I want to clear things up and go together.

- Current approach and how it's working: Silent treatment and I am avoiding him. Not working because I miss my friend.

- What do you think the other person is feeling? Angry and frustrated at me.

Let's put this into the first verse of the song:

I know we had an argument last night
And now we're not talking
You must be angry and frustrated with me
I'm just avoiding it all

Chorus
(of *Peaceful Easy Feeling*)

3. Now it's your turn to go back to your situation and write verse one. Think back to DEAR MAN and approach with GIVE. GIVE is perhaps the way you would naturally talk with a friend—asking gently, listening with interest, and repeating back to them what you hear them say. But when there is a conflict, this doesn't necessarily come as easily to us. So it takes practice and going back to DEAR MAN and adding GIVE. This gives you clarity and you're more likely to ask in an effective manner.

Being aware of what the conflict is, how it makes you feel, and what you think the other person is feeling can give you ideas for how to write out what you could say to this person you have conflict with using the DEAR MAN GIVE skill. For example:

D: We had an argument last night and we are avoiding each other.

E: I miss you.

A: I'm afraid you're angry, but I still want us to talk. Will you give me a ride to the event so we can talk on our way?

R: We will be able to hash out the argument and be friends again.

M: I'll stay on track with what I want.

A: I won't avoid, and will ask despite his response.

N: We can negotiate for other options.

G: I won't yell, be gentle.

I: I will act interested and look him in the eye.

V: I will look at his side, listen closely as he speaks, and repeat what I heard him say.

E: I will stay calm and breathe.

Now we can turn these lines into verses that go with the song.

D: I know we had an argument last night
And now we're not talking
E: I really miss you cuz you're my best friend
I'd like to see you tonight
A: I'm afraid you're angry, but I still want us to talk
Will you give me a ride tonight
R: We can talk as we travel there
And clear this whole thing up

G: I won't yell, I'll be gentle
I: I'll act interested and look you in the eye
V: I'll hear your side and listen closely as you speak
E: I will stay calm and breathe

Chorus
(of *Peaceful Easy Feeling*)

ACTION STEP FOR THIS WEEK

1. Think of something you want to ask someone for where the relationship with the person is important to you. It could be that you want to ask someone out to the movies, and your choice of movie is different than theirs. It could be that you want to ask your boss for a raise. Using the format above, write out a DEAR MAN script with GIVE on a sheet of paper.

2. Try it with someone. Practice using the skill.

Congratulations! You have completed this activity/lesson! Celebrate by sharing your biggest takeaway with a friend or your therapist, or through journaling. It's going to lock in what you learned today.

KEEPING YOUR SELF-RESPECT (FAST)

FAST is the skill to use when your self-respect is the most important priority in the interpersonal situation. Ask yourself, "How do I want to feel about myself at the end of this interaction?" If you suspect that you may feel poorly about yourself due to being too passive or too aggressive, use the FAST skill to walk away feeling more self-respect.

F: Fair

Be fair to yourself and the other person.

A: No Apologies

If an apology is warranted, use one; otherwise don't. Don't apologize for saying no or for asking. Let's say you lent some money to a friend and are asking for it back. Don't say, "You owe me money, I'm sorry for asking for it." No. You deserve it. That was the agreement. You have the right to ask for it and receive it back.

S: Stick to Your Values

Do what you know is right. If someone asks you to do something that feels wrong to you, say no. If your friend asks you to steal and that is against your values, say no. If you are a vegetarian and are offered a meat meal, say no. It's your right.

T: Be Truthful

At times, one may feel uncomfortable sharing our needs or saying no, so we "bend" the truth or make up excuses. "Be Truthful" is just being honest with yourself and others. Your needs, requests, and desires are valid.

Instructions

1. Listen to the song *NO* by Meghan Trainor. While you listen, notice if she is using the FAST skill.

Was she fair?

_____

Did she apologize?

_____

Did she stick to her values?

_____

Was she truthful?

_____

If you think she wasn't using the skill, or any part of it, what do you think needs to be changed and how?

_____

2. What things are important to you that you value? For example:

    I'm a vegetarian

    I don't steal

    I value honesty

    I value people who take showers

    I value music

3. List ten of your values:

    1.

    2.

    3.

    4.

    5.

    6.

    7.

    8.

9.

10.

4. Think of a time that you wanted to say no to something because it was against your values. Or imagine a situation that if it happened you would feel it crossed your line. Write out the script of what you could say to the person.

D

E

A

R

M

A

N

F

A

S

T

ACTION STEP FOR THIS WEEK

1. Try using the FAST skill with someone. Practice using it.

2. Do something creative with your values, e.g., a collage or a painting, and share them in a letter (or an email or text) to a friend.

Congratulations! You have completed this activity/lesson! Celebrate by sharing your biggest takeaway with a friend or your therapist, or through journaling. It's going to lock in what you learned today.

UNIT 5: WALKING THE MIDDLE PATH

LESSONS

- Dialectics

- Validation

- Increase Desired Behaviors and Decrease Undesired Behaviors

DIALECTICS
What Is a Dialectic?

A dialectic is when two things that seem to be opposite are both true at the same time. The sun may be shining bright and hot, and the temperature outside can be cold. You can both love someone and disagree with them.

We are tempted to see people, situations, and choices as right or wrong; consider that there is a middle path where both can be true.

Tip: Language matters! Pay attention to your use of the word "but" and try and replace it instead with the word "and." Also, try to stay away from the words "always" and "never." They are inherently non-dialectical!

Instructions

1. Listen to a piece of classical music (e.g., *Songs Without Words* by Mendelssohn). While you listen, create two watercolor paintings that are inspired by the piece. As the music ends, name each painting with an emotion word. Are they the same? How could the same piece of music evoke or lead you to different emotions? Dialectics show us that there is more than one way to view an experience—even ourselves.

2. Listen to the song *Hand in My Pocket* by Alanis Morissette and write down five dialectics she identifies about herself.

_____

_____

_____

_____

_____

ACTION STEP FOR THIS WEEK

Make a list of at least five dialectics about yourself and/or about yourself in conflict with another person. For example: "I am strong *and* I am soft hearted," and "It's important to me to stay out until midnight with my friends so I can connect more with them *and* my mother wants me home by 11pm because she believes it's important that I get enough sleep."

Substitute your list into the lyrics of the song and sing it to yourself.

Congratulations! You have completed this activity/lesson! Celebrate by sharing your biggest takeaway with a friend or your therapist, or through journaling. It's going to lock in what you learned today.

VALIDATION

Validation is acknowledging that a person's experiences, for example, their thoughts, emotions, urges, or behaviors, are valid or make sense in some way. Feeling heard, or allowing another person to feel heard, is validating! You don't have to agree with someone to validate their experience, and they don't have to agree with you to validate yours.

When we are told that what we are feeling, thinking, or doing is wrong, when we feel ignored, misunderstood, unheard, and belittled, it's called invalidation. Invalidation can be painful.

Tip: Be careful to validate *only* the valid and not the invalid! For example, if my best friend yells at me because she's on edge and angry from failing an important test, I would *not* validate her yelling at me. Instead I would validate that it makes sense to feel angry when you believe you deserve a better grade.

Instructions

1. Listen to the songs *When You're Smiling* by Dean Martin and *True Colors* by Cyndi Lauper (also recorded by Anna Kendrick and Justin Timberlake).

2. Find the lyrics to both of these songs and write them out.

3. Identify which song has validating lyrics and which has invalidating lyrics.

4. Can you think of other songs whose lyrics are either validating or invalidating?

5. Can you think of a time when someone said something to you that was invalidating? What was it? How did it make you feel and think about yourself?

    For example: The other day I painted the walls in my office. My friend said, "Wow, you painted your office *that* color? You painted this wall really unevenly too," and laughed while saying this. Immediately I felt shame and had the thought, "He thinks I'm a horrible painter!" I could have internalized this comment further by thinking and believing, "I should quit while I'm ahead. I'll never be able to finish it nicely. I'm a failure..." This is an example of turning invalidation by others into self-invalidation!

The example in the song, *When You're Smiling*, assumes that if a person is crying, that's a bad thing and no one would want to be around it, so cheer up. If I take this message to heart, I ignore my true colors (as in the other song).

Self-Validation

Just as important as learning how to validate others is learning how to validate ourselves. Using skills such as Check the Facts, Non-Judgmentalness, and Self-Soothing, can help us see the validity in our feelings, thoughts, and experiences.

In the examples above I realized that the paint I used in this room was a different quality of paint than what I had used in the other rooms. Additionally, the other rooms turned out looking really nice! Therefore, believing I'm a bad painter is both judgmental and not acknowledging all of the facts. I Checked the Facts and Problem Solved by buying better-quality paint. My alternative thought was saying to myself, "I'm not a failure. I did the best job possible with the paint I had."

Referring back to the lyrics in *When You're Smiling*, crying was invalidated. When I'm crying, there are ways I can Self-Soothe, accept my emotions, and learn from them. Crying lets me know that I am in pain and can problem solve and/or seek support if needed.

ACTION STEP FOR THIS WEEK

Notice when you feel invalidated by another, or make invalidating statements towards yourself or other people ("I am so stupid," or "That girl is so crazy!" for example) and take steps towards validating others and self-validation ("I'm having the thought that I'm stupid. What I did was an honest mistake. I am learning every day and one mistake does not define me.").

Congratulations! You have completed this activity/lesson! Celebrate by sharing your biggest takeaway with a friend or your therapist, or through journaling. It's going to lock in what you learned today.

INCREASE DESIRED BEHAVIORS AND DECREASE UNDESIRED BEHAVIORS

Making change can be uncomfortable and seem challenging. Habits can be hard to break. We can increase the likelihood of success through reinforcing and shaping the behaviors we want to strengthen. Success can start with identifying what you want to change and what you find rewarding.

One strategy you can use to increase effective behaviors is positive reinforcement.

Identify one behavior that you want to increase:

_____

Now we have to identify the reinforcer...

What sounds are pleasing to you?

_____

What songs do you love to listen to?

_____

Every time you engage in the more effective behavior, the one that you want to increase, reward yourself with the reinforcer (e.g., a song you love or a sound that is pleasing to you) immediately after. This will encourage you to engage in this behavior more often in order to get the reinforcer!

One strategy that you can use to decrease ineffective behaviors is punishment.

Identify a behavior you would like to decrease:

_____

What sound do you find distressing and would want to avoid?

_____

What songs do you hate to listen to?

_____

Every time you engage in the behavior that you want to decrease, listen to a song you hate or a sound you want to avoid, and notice if this encourages you to lessen that behavior.

In this exercise, music and sound are used as the reward or the punishment—tools to help change our behavior and shape it to be the way we want it to be.

Tip: Reinforcement works better than punishment, so make sure you spend more time thinking of behaviors you'd like to increase rather than the opposite. For example, if you eat a lot of junk food and want to reduce this behavior, instead of punishing yourself every time you have junk food, reward yourself every time you have a healthy snack!

ACTION STEP FOR THIS WEEK

1. List additional music, sounds, or tools that can serve as rewards or deterrents.

2. List habits you would like to increase or decrease.

3. Practice challenging your habits.

Congratulations! You have completed this activity/lesson! Celebrate by sharing your biggest takeaway with a friend or your therapist, or through journaling. It's going to lock in what you learned today.

CONGRATULATIONS!

You have worked through the modules and started learning the skills!

Building a life worth living incorporates consistent learning and practice (Building Mastery). Here are some ideas to strengthen your wellness.

1. Print out the skills summary pages to keep a visual reminder and help track your use.

2. Journal each day about a skill you used or could have used.

3. Rework the program.

4. Teach a skill to someone else.

5. Create your own song, jingle, or chant for your favorite skill or for the skill you need the most.

6. Keep a log of skills used throughout the week and reward yourself for using a targeted number of skills.

7. Read more about DBT. Be curious and ask questions. Seek guidance from a DBT program or resource if needed or desired.

FURTHER RESOURCES

SONGS
The following songs are downloadable from www.jkp.com/voucher using the code HUUWAHE.

- *DEAR MAN*
- *The Roller Coaster Ride*
- *The Message*
- *The System Song*
- *I'm Gonna Make It*
- *Pros and Cons*

BOOKS
Linehan, M. M. (2015). *DBT Skills Training Manual, 2nd edition.* New York, NY: Guilford Press.
Rathus, J. H., & Miller, A. L. (2015). *DBT Skills Manual for Adolescents.* New York, NY: Guilford Press.

WEBSITES
For details about the workshop that accompanies this book visit: dbtmusic.com
Behavioral Tech (DBT organization): www.behavioraltech.com
American Music Therapy Association: www.musictherapy.org
For more information on workshops, classes, and research: TheSpiegelAcademy.com

References

American Music Therapy Association (1998–2019). *What is Music Therapy?* Accessed on 5/8/2019 at www.musictherapy.org/about/musictherapy/.

Linehan, M. M. (2015). *DBT Skills Training Manual, 2nd edition.* New York, NY: Guilford Press.

Mind Tools (1996–2019). *Using Affirmations.* Accessed on 6/8/2019 at www.mindtools.com/pages/article/affirmations.htm.

Niebuhr, R. (1951). *Spirituality and Alternative Healing.* Accessed on 9/8/2019 at http://skdesigns.com/internet/articles/prose/niebuhr/serenity_prayer/.

Rathus, J. H., & Miller, A. L. (2015). *DBT Skills Manual for Adolescents.* New York, NY: Guilford Press.